CAUSES & CURES

in the CLASSROOM

ASCD MEMBER BOOK

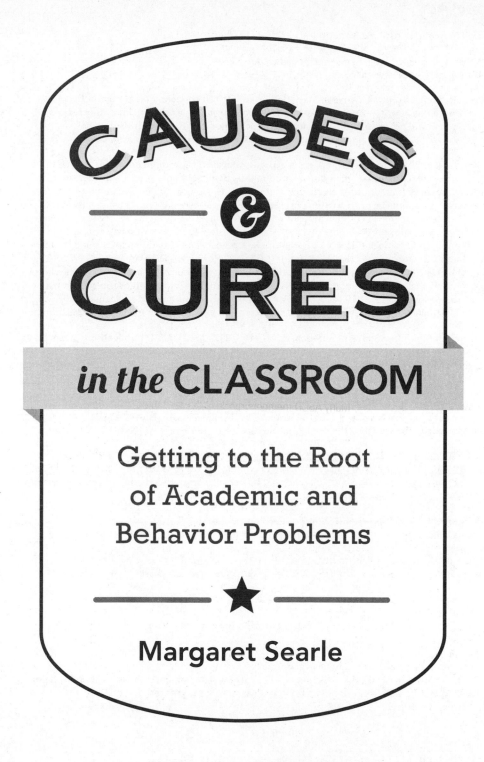

CAUSES & CURES

in the CLASSROOM

Getting to the Root of Academic and Behavior Problems

★

Margaret Searle

ASCD Alexandria, VA USA

1703 N. Beauregard St. • Alexandria, VA 22311-1714 USA
Phone: 800-933-2723 or 703-578-9600 • Fax: 703-575-5400
Website: www.ascd.org • E-mail: member@ascd.org
Author guidelines: www.ascd.org/write

Gene R. Carter, *Executive Director;* Mary Catherine (MC) Desrosiers, *Chief Program Development Officer;* Richard Papale, *Publisher;* Genny Ostertag, *Acquisitions Editor;* Julie Houtz, *Director, Book Editing & Production;* Miriam Goldstein, *Editor;* Lindsey Smith, *Graphic Designer;* Mike Kalyan, *Production Manager;* Keith Demmons, *Desktop Publishing Specialist*

All web links in this book are correct as of the publication date below but may have become inactive or otherwise modified since that time. If you notice a deactivated or changed link, please e-mail books@ascd.org with the words "Link Update" in the subject line. In your message, please specify the web link, the book title, and the page number on which the link appears.

ASCD Member Book No. FY14-2 (Nov. 2013, PSI+). ASCD Member Books mail to Premium (P), Select (S), and Institutional Plus (I+) members on this schedule: Jan., PSI+; Feb., P; Apr., PSI+; May, P; July, PSI+; Aug., P; Sept., PSI+; Nov., PSI+; Dec., P. For up-to-date details on membership, see www.ascd.org/membership.

PAPERBACK ISBN: 978-1-4166-1632-0   ASCD product #113019
Also available as an e-book (see Books in Print for the ISBNs).

Quantity discounts: 10–49 copies, 10%; 50+ copies, 15%; for 1,000 or more copies, call 800-933-2723, ext. 5634, or 703-575-5634. For desk copies: www.ascd.org/deskcopy

Library of Congress Cataloging-in-Publication Data
Searle, Margaret.
  Causes & cures in the classroom : getting to the root of academic and behavior problems / Margaret Searle.
    pages cm
  Includes bibliographical references and index.
    ISBN 978-1-4166-1632-0 (pbk. : alk. paper) 1. Learning disabled children–Education. 2. Learning disabled children–Behavior modification. 3. Classroom management. I. Title.
    LC4704.S43 2013
    371.102'4–dc23
                          2013029607

23 22 21 20 19 18 17 16 15 14 13   1 2 3 4 5 6 7 8 9 10 11 12

To my children, Morgan and Kenton, who have grounded Michael and me in the reality of what it takes to guide and support children as they travel the road to becoming caring and responsible adults.

CAUSES & CURES

in the CLASSROOM

ACKNOWLEDGMENTS

I owe a debt of gratitude to all the teams of teachers and administrators who contributed their ideas and suggestions to help shape the content and case studies for this book. Special thanks to my husband Michael, Debbie Siegel, Joan Love, and Marilyn Swartz for their ongoing input and critiques.

Thanks also to Genny Ostertag, who helped me wrap my mind around the ideas for this book, and Miriam Goldstein, whose editing skills crafted my draft into a more readable and consistent flow of ideas.

INTRODUCTION

Whether our students leave our classrooms confident and goal-directed or frustrated and unfulfilled depends on our ability to do two things: diagnose their needs and deliver support. This dual challenge is daunting, especially if students come to school with weak vocabulary, shallow experience bases, and poor planning and organization skills. Our job becomes even more mind-boggling when students' brain development causes problems with memory, impulse control, and attention span.

Faced with such complicating issues, teachers often become baffled by what to do next. Many times, I have heard teachers say they have exhausted all the possibilities: "What can I do with a student who turns in half of her work, can't remember what we covered the day before, and insists on being the class clown? I have tried everything." The truth is, a teacher may have tried everything he or she already knows to do, but teaching hard-to-reach students often demands a broader perspective and base of knowledge and experience than one person can bring to bear. Teachers often struggle to solve tough student issues alone, when the magnitude of the problem calls for the support of a team of professionals and a solid framework for decision making. In this book, I lay out a problem-solving protocol as well as practical interventions designed to help teams diagnose needs and deliver the best support to their students.

Causes & Cures is a guide for all educators. K–12 teachers, psychologists, administrators, and student service providers can all benefit from the book's problem-solving process and apply it to any type of behavioral or academic problem at any grade level. The process and action options described in the following chapters take into account findings from both academic and neurological research and make the book much more than a simple listing of accommodations and interventions. The five-step protocol will lead you from observed problem or behavior to root causes to goals and intervention plans. You can use the same process when addressing problems at building and district levels, although the examples in this book focus on individual student issues, with some suggestions for large-group applications. Let's look at an encapsulation of the protocol.

The Five Basic Steps of Problem Solving

1. *Know the traits of the student or group to be supported.* Teachers identify not only concerns about students but also student strengths. This balanced approach clarifies baseline data that will help in determining ways to measure the effectiveness of the interventions chosen.
2. *Analyze the root causes.* The strategy I recommend for this step is called the "Five Whys" analysis. This questioning technique is based on Toyota's quality tools and is designed to go beyond symptoms to identify root causes.
3. *Set clear and measurable goals.* Measurable goals focus the action plan and serve as the basis for monitoring growth.
4. *Decide how to monitor and chart the student's progress.* Close monitoring of student progress guides decisions. We know whether to adjust or fade the action plan based on results we see.
5. *Compose intervention options and select a plan.* The template used for this step serves as a guide for identifying viable research-based accommodation and intervention possibilities for action plans. Parents, the student, and faculty work together to select the ideas that are best suited to the identified student needs (Searle, 2007).

These five steps have helped hundreds of teachers solve difficult student problems, but the process is not for the faint of heart. Depending on how well your faculty already works in teams and willingly spends time searching for new approaches, this system may require some fundamental shifts in how you do business.

What Will Move Us Forward

To tackle tough student issues effectively, we must examine and update our traditional practices. Three big changes are often needed to avoid the most common pitfalls in addressing student problems.

1. *Focus on what blocks student learning* before concentrating on which intervention to use. Grabbing a list of strategies and beginning interventions without taking the time to figure out the root causes of problems looks like a tempting shortcut but is an inefficient use of teacher time and energy that often results in high frustration.
2. *Minimize the guessing factor by staying informed* on current brain and educational research. Research helps identify common core causes as well as strategies proven to be effective for many students. Faculties often complain when asked to use team time to read and discuss research, but this step minimizes time wasted applying the wrong interventions to the wrong student for the wrong amount of time.
3. *Train for and monitor the implementation of interventions.* Professional development is needed for teachers to understand how strategies must be implemented to see a significant change in achievement. If research says the strategy works well when implemented in small-group instruction three days a week for four weeks in 20-minute sessions, we shouldn't be surprised when it doesn't show results after two weeks of 10-minute sessions done in a large group.

Implementation with fidelity is critical, and teachers need feedback from team members to make certain they are correctly interpreting what the research says. We are not talking about reinventing the wheel. Many effective strategies will be techniques some teachers already know about and use regularly. A team approach is fundamental to building capacity as all faculty members share ideas and support one another.

As Doug Reeves (2009) points out, working smarter with a new focus may create anxiety for some teachers and outright negativity on the part of others, but we must stay the course if we want positive results. Administrators and team leaders must address the issue of time and collaboration as teachers develop new skills. A proactive rather than a reactive approach to training and support is critical. We cannot become masterful at what we do when collaborative data meetings, critical conversations, and constructive feedback are considered invasions of privacy or low priorities on the school schedule. Figure A presents some important points to consider as you implement this problem-solving method.

What's Ahead

Each chapter of this book addresses a specific area of behavior and academic problems and provides a case study that will walk you through the five problem-solving steps. Clear examples of individual student issues in a variety of subject areas and grade levels are the focus, but keep in mind that these models can be applied to groups as well as individuals.

Chapter 1 introduces new neurological research about possible root causes of many academic and behavior issues. We now know that delays in the maturity of brain processes known as executive functions can be at the core of what previously were often thought to be attitude and behavior problems. Without receiving support for these delayed functions, some students can try their hardest and still be unsuccessful in school.

Chapter 2 focuses on ways to support students who have trouble with planning and problem solving. Some of these students' key difficulties are initiating and finishing work, persevering when tasks get hard or boring, managing time, and self-monitoring. The academic area of emphasis is social studies.

Chapter 3 explores ways to merge executive function support and academic interventions needed by students who struggle with math because of poor memory skills and their inability to visualize and solve complex problems.

Chapter 4 discusses students whose poor organization and writing skills are causing both their grades and their self-confidence to suffer.

A | What This Problem-Solving Method Is and What It Is Not

It Is	It Is Not
It is teamwork. Team members learn from one another. They make time to hear and see what master teachers who work down the hall are doing to get results. They also study and share what teachers who have participated in research studies are doing. ·	**It is not trying to solve problems in isolation.** A team must continuously monitor student progress data to see which interventions match a specific student's or group's needs. Multiple perspectives help with the development of solid plans and adjustments based on data.
It is learning to diagnose deeply by investing time and effort. This skill requires finding time for learning to do the "Five Whys" analysis as well as time for reading and discussing brain and educational research. Finding team time to do this is difficult but will pay off a hundredfold in the long run.	**It is not assuming the obvious skill deficits are the core causes of student problems.** Using data and research to identify core causes of problems is the quickest and most efficient path to solving them.
It is analyzing which strategies are effective. This requires becoming increasingly savvy in identifying when and with whom given interventions are likely to work based on the diagnosed root causes.	**It is not using random interventions.** Simply trying a series of interventions from a website or reference book without first analyzing both the students' academic needs and their executive function skills wastes time and energy.
It is going beyond the one-size-fits-all approach for intervening and assessing. Even the best interventions are not equally effective for all types of students with the same symptoms, so the team must consider a variety of assessments and interventions.	**It is not grouping based on low performance.** We do not necessarily need another layer of testing, nor should we group kids by high, average, and low performance. We need to use our best assessment information to see why the problem persists in spite of our efforts and use short-term grouping based on specific needs.
It is a way of rethinking. Sometimes the typical approaches to age-old problems of student achievement, motivation, attention span, and behavior are not the most effective.	**It is not another program added to teachers' workloads.** If this process is done well, it will actually save instructional time and increase the focus on improving student learning.

Chapter 5 concentrates on students whose weak attention and focusing skills interfere with reading comprehension and social skills.

Chapter 6 addresses causes and solutions for students who have difficulty controlling themselves at school. Science is the academic content example for this chapter.

Chapters 2 through 6 conclude with an "On Your Own" section that invites you to work through the five-step problem-solving process with a case study student. To facilitate the process, you can download blank forms for each step at www.ascd .org/ASCD/pdf/books/searlefivesteps2013.pdf. Use the password "searle113019" to unlock the PDF.

My hope is that no matter what content or grade level you teach, you will see how each step of this process can help you maximize your potential to make a difference in the lives of your students.

1

WHAT IS EXECUTIVE FUNCTION AND HOW DOES IT AFFECT SCHOOL PERFORMANCE?

Barry is getting an F in social studies and science mostly because he doesn't hand his assignments in on time, if at all. His note-taking skills during lectures are a disaster. His mind wanders, and when he does manage to be attentive, he tries to write down everything. He often has trouble separating important from unimportant information. He also has a hard time remembering directions or steps in a process.

Jolene can't seem to stop doing things that disrupt the classroom. Keeping her body in the same vicinity as her desk takes all the willpower she can muster. She shouts out answers and pushes peers who annoy her. When it's time to work, her attention is everywhere except on the assignment. She makes the same mistakes in math over and over, even though her teacher has reviewed the processes with her multiple times.

Amy seldom arrives to class on time, and it is the rare day when she manages to remember to bring all of the books, supplies, and assignments she needs. She sits and stares instead of getting started on her work. The quality of the written work Amy does produce is marginal, even though she can answer questions orally as well as anyone. Her tendency is to give up when the work gets challenging, and she rarely checks her assignments before handing them in.

Each of these students may sound like a candidate for special education testing, and it is possible that they have learning disabilities, but there is also another possibility. Many typical students who have delays in executive function exhibit exactly these same symptoms.

What Is Executive Function?

Executive function is the term used by neurologists to describe the brain processes that drive our ability to focus, solve problems, organize ourselves, remember information, learn from mistakes, and manage impulses, all of which help us learn efficiently and develop important social skills (Blair, 2002).

Dr. Russell Barkley and Dr. Thomas Brown, noted researchers in the area of attention deficit disorder (ADD), use the analogy of an orchestra conductor to describe the brain's executive function. A conductor's job is to direct each member of the orchestra in order to create the most beautiful sound possible. No matter how talented the musicians, if the conductor doesn't keep the pace and intensity of the playing coordinated, the result can be ugly. If our brain's conductor is underactive, we will have the same outcome: the lack of focus and integration will cause us to perform poorly (Barkley, Murphy, & Fischer, 2008).

During the last 20 years, neuroscientists have made remarkable progress in understanding how the brain works, but we are just beginning to realize how crucial this information can be for parents and educators. Understanding how executive skills develop can help adults figure out the best responses to academic and behavioral problems that are often mistaken for laziness, carelessness, or lack of motivation.

We know there is wide disparity in people's capacity to manage executive skills. This disparity is especially noticeable in children because the prefrontal cortex is in a constant and uneven state of development.

The Maturation Process

Compare your ability to plan, manage time, maintain focus, and control impulses with that of a 5-year-old. Although 5-year-olds are beginning to handle these tasks, natural maturation of the brain and experience make adults quicker and more efficient. Executive functioning skills, such as predicting what is likely to happen next, solving complex problems, and judging when and how long to work on a project, become easier for us as the brain matures.

Studies show that even though the executive processes start developing in infancy, these cognitive skills develop at different rates and over a long period. The skills of inhibition (overriding automatic responses) and working memory (holding information long enough to work with it) are the first to show significant growth in preschool children. Planning, attention span, and organization show a spike in development around age 5 but don't peak until our mid- to late 20s. During the adolescent years, all of these brain systems become faster and more sophisticated, and the skills of self-monitoring, mental flexibility, and persistence become noticeably stronger (Diamond, 2002).

The level of a child's executive function skills is not highly predictable by age because the developmental rate of the prefrontal cortex, which governs the function, can vary by a large degree from person to person. Some students may have skills that seem behind or ahead of the rest of the class, and as we have seen in the examples at the opening of this chapter, the problems that manifest can easily be interpreted as signs of a possible disability or lack of effort. Before jumping to testing, labeling, or punishing, it is important to try supporting students with interventions for various executive skills like organization, self-monitoring, multitasking, and memory. Many students get mislabeled as students with disabilities when what they really need is ongoing support while their brains go through the normal maturation process.

Contrary to popular belief, it is the level of executive function skills, especially in the area of working memory, rather than IQ that is the best predictor of success in reading, spelling, and math (Alloway & Alloway, 2010). Classroom teachers often describe struggling children as being inattentive or as having low IQ, but rarely do they put their finger on working memory and related executive subskills as the key reasons for poor performance. The good news is that these skills, unlike IQ, are easily addressed in school with early interventions in the classroom.

Although executive control has little to do with a person's IQ, the likelihood is high that students with cognitive disabilities will have difficulties in several areas of executive functioning (Brown, 2005). Barkley's research (Barkley et al., 2008) reported that 89–98 percent of children diagnosed as having ADD have deficits in multiple areas of executive function. This means that students with disabilities can be as much as three years behind their peers in some aspects of executive maturity. Ask a room full of special education teachers if their students experience problems with organization, memory, and attention span, and every hand in the room will go up. But ask a room of middle school general education teachers the same question, and you will find that students with disabilities aren't the only ones who struggle in these areas.

Genetics, disabilities, stage of life, gender, quality of family life, self-concept, and stress levels affect the natural timeline for the development of executive functioning. Life experiences, good nutrition, and sensitive adult guidance also contribute to how well and how fast these problem-solving and self-regulation abilities mature. The good news is there are many things parents and educators can do to nurture the executive skills of students with disabilities and general education students alike.

We can help students feel more capable by adjusting expectations to offer enough challenge to keep growth and interest high without crossing the line into frustration. Providing the right amount of modeling and support, based on what we know about a student's stage of brain development, establishes a safe and welcoming environment for growth. When punishment instead of support is our response, we can actually stall the developmental process.

The Six Major Subskills of Executive Function

Although *executive control* or *executive function* may not be well-known terms to many teachers, the traits and frustrations caused by delays in these processing skills are very familiar. There is disagreement among neurologists about what to call the subskills that make up executive function, but in this book, I concentrate on six categories: planning and problem solving, memory, organization, focusing attention, impulse control, and self-monitoring.

These functions are so closely related that it is often hard to separate one from the other. For example, if you miss your doctor's appointment, is it because your planning is faulty, or could it be your memory that let you down? If you say something that hurts someone's feelings, is it because you aren't paying attention to the social cues the person is sending, is it due to a lack of impulse control, or could it be poor problem solving? It's hard to tell. A deficit in a particular skill can be difficult to pinpoint because usually the problem is due to a combination of skill factors. However, for the purposes of clarity, in this book, I treat each of the executive skills as if it operated in isolation. Let's take a closer look at each of these six functions and the problems you are likely to see if students' development in a particular one is delayed.

Planning and Problem Solving

Tyler has known about the math project for a week, and it's due tomorrow. Mom will hit the ceiling again when she checks his notebook tonight. He wants to do well in school, but whenever he gets long, complicated assignments, his brain goes into a stall. He cannot imagine where to begin, so he doesn't. It never occurs to him to ask for help.

To help you better identify with Tyler's problems, let's transfer his executive dysfunction to an adult scenario and pretend that you too have delayed development of your planning and problem-solving skills. What happens to you now? Well, like Tyler, you will frequently get lost in the goal setting and visualization of steps required for good work completion. A complex task like balancing your checkbook freaks you out. Your inability to break this big task into manageable parts makes the job look overwhelming and distasteful, so you tend to put it off. Now you find yourself sitting with three months' worth of receipts and bank statements in front of you, and you just can't bring yourself to get started because you cannot imagine where to begin. If you do get under way and something doesn't work out, you can't think of a plan B. It's easier to just say, "I simply can't do this," and so you stop.

Many students with faulty problem-solving skills are repeatedly unsuccessful in getting started or meeting goals and accessing resources, which can lead them to become more and more reluctant to set and stick with goals that challenge them. They begin to think they are not as smart or capable as other people. To avoid this downward spiral, adults need to consider the possibility that the lack of initiative may be due to executive dysfunction. If this is true, the problem is an "I can't" rather than an "I won't" issue, and support, not punishment, is what is needed.

The experience of feeling overwhelmed by complex problems is understandable, but it's risky to allow the pattern of not getting started or not following through to become a habit. Without direct support, this problem is likely to happen repeatedly, even when there are severe consequences. You will find a variety of specific suggestions for supporting the skills of problem solving and planning in Chapter 2.

When planning and problem solving is causing trouble, there is generally a related issue in the memory system.

Memory

Amber's teacher repeatedly reminds her to put her name and date at the top of her paper, but Amber forgets to do this at least once a day. If there are several steps involved in solving the math problem, she is likely to remember the first and the last step but skip the steps in between. Even though Amber demonstrates that she understands basic grammar, spelling, and punctuation when doing practice exercises, she has difficulty remembering how to apply these rules when she is actually writing.

Now, let's put you in Amber's shoes for a moment. If, like Amber's, your memory processes don't function effectively, holding information in your mind long enough to do something with it is difficult. You cannot remember the rules of a game as you play it. People refer to you as absentminded or careless because you frequently forget to do things like go to appointments or pay bills on time. You come home from the grocery store without some of the things you need. You have trouble following multistep directions or instructions. You can't tell a story with enough detail or in proper sequence for people to follow your thoughts easily. Remembering a phone number or a person's name is frustrating. In short, life is much more exasperating for you than it is for other people.

Students who have weak executive memory systems experience these frustrations regularly. Memory dysfunction affects not only their ability to learn, communicate, and problem-solve but also their social and emotional well-being. For example, students with weak memory are less likely to feel comfortable responding in class and are more likely to "zone out" when the tasks or conversations are demanding. They are frequently in trouble for not following directions. Often teachers also identify these students as having oppositional and hyperactive tendencies.

The memory function is highly complex, and actually not one function but many. Scientists break memory processes down into three types: encoding (intake system), working memory (processing), and long-term memory (storage and retrieval).

Encoding is the process by which the brain takes in new sensory stimuli and compares and associates them with prior memories in order to create new memories. The more we focus our attention on the stimuli, the stronger the encoding. The more personally meaningful the sensory information or the more emotion we feel when processing it, the stronger the memory. That is why you probably cannot remember what you had for lunch on Wednesday three weeks ago, unless it was a special occasion on which you either had the best meal ever or became deathly ill afterward. The more difficult it is for you to understand the incoming information, the weaker and more distorted the encoding.

Students who have difficulty with encoding often *can't*

- Sort out what information to focus on.
- Keep up with the pace of the information, so they zone in and out.
- Focus on information they don't find engaging or challenging.
- Link new information to what they already know.
- Easily use an intake system (auditory, visual, kinesthetic) other than their strongest.
- Follow directions, because they gloss over details and sequences.
- Learn easily from previous mistakes.

Notice that the word *can't* is the operative word here. These problems are not just the result of carelessness. Even when these students give their best effort, it simply is not enough. The same is true for students with delays in processing information in working memory.

Working memory is what we use to link information together into meaningful chunks so that we can carry out important mental tasks, like comparing, sequencing, summarizing, filtering out irrelevant information, reading, and solving problems. When the working memory process misfires, it causes those "Oops, what did I come in here to get?" moments. Working memory's short-term storage must hold our purpose in mind long enough to perform more complex processes.

Students with working memory issues often take longer to make sense of things and may be *unable* to

- Follow through on directions, even when they understand them.
- Remember where they are in a process when doing multistep procedures or tasks.
- Remember what they just read long enough to make connections to other information.
- Detect patterns, relationships, and the logic of situations.
- Apply previous knowledge to new events, or predict or imagine future events.

Long-term memory relies on a person's ability to make connections and categorize information by linking it to prior knowledge. We file information according to its similarity to something we already know, and we retrieve information according to its difference from the information we filed it with. Students with storage and retrieval weaknesses may have a hard time in one or both processes. Typically, even though these students might understand the information perfectly as they hear it, they may not be able to get it out of long-term storage when they need it.

Students with delays in storage and retrieval skills may be *unable* to

- Match sounds with letters, or symbols with numbers.
- Transfer or apply a skill to an unfamiliar situation or problem.
- Follow through on directions and commitments.
- Evaluate new information for relevance or effectiveness.
- Remain calm in a testing situation.
- Comprehend while reading or listening.

All of these memory skills typically improve with maturity, but quality instruction and support increase the success rate while executive functions are developing. One way to support memory is to build multiple pathways for taking in and practicing new information. For example, when learning to play a game, if you can see a person model the process as you listen to the directions, the learning is stronger, especially if you can then try a practice round before you actually start playing. This sets up auditory, visual, and kinesthetic pathways for memory storage and retrieval. Chapter 3 covers specific examples of useful student interventions for developing stronger memory systems.

A stronger memory will increase students' chances of being able to improve their organizational skills, because they can remember patterns for sorting and categorizing.

Organization

"Unreliable and sloppy" is how Jake's teachers often describe him, and he is beginning to believe these labels are true. He wants to do well, but he always runs out of time. Every morning starts out as a game of hide-and-seek. He keeps his inventory of clothes in a heap on the floor, and his book bag could be anywhere in the house. After he shoots out the door, he remembers that he didn't have Mom sign his permission slip for the field trip. This is going to be another rough day. Even when he promises to do better, he finds himself slipping back into his old habits of "I'll organize this later" thinking.

Now, let's make your capacity for organization as poor as Jake's so that you share his cluttered thinking and lack of insight about the logical consequences of disorganization. You can't remember where you put the tool you need even though you just used it yesterday. You find yourself paying credit card bills without veri-fying the amount owed because you wouldn't take the time to double-check all those receipts even if you could find them. People refer to you as scatterbrained because your mind skips from one activity to another as you work. At the end of the day, you often find that you have started seven projects and finished none. If sorting and organizing were a sport, no one would pick you for their team. The frustration of keeping track of your time, space, and materials makes simple jobs much harder for you than they should be.

Everyone experiences moments of disorganization. Under pressure, we all revert to what feels right, even when it isn't. But for students with executive delays, the situation is much worse. They seldom see the reasons for their mistakes, so they don't learn from them even when told repeatedly how to fix the problems. To make any long-term change, students with poorly developed organizational thinking need much more modeling and practice than most in order to develop habits that feel right (Hattie, Biggs, & Purdie, 1996).

Getting organized is one thing; staying organized is quite another. Using visual organizers, providing corrective feedback, and scheduling enough time for organiz-ing before the end of class help students develop new habits. I examine more specific interventions for supporting organization and follow-through in Chapter 4.

When students are not thriving academically or behaviorally, the lack of ability to focus attention may be what triggers planning, memory, and organization problems.

Focusing Attention

Tamra finds it impossible to concentrate for long periods of time, but when she takes a break, her brain cannot seem to refocus. She tunes in and out during class and misses critical details in her notes. She can't resist the temptation to turn on her music while doing homework even though she knows it affects her ability to concentrate. Tamra works hard but is discouraged because she doesn't seem to accomplish much.

You probably have had trouble keeping focus at times, especially if you were tired, hungry, stressed, or bored, but what if you experienced the daily problems with focusing attention that a delay in this executive function might cause? What if you had Tamra's attention span? Your mind would wander during conversations, and you would have to reread the same passage several times in order to comprehend it.

If you didn't take frequent breaks, your brain would take them for you. People would refer to you as careless because of your tendency to overlook details and do things like forget to put sugar in the cookie batter. If your child cut herself and was bleeding, you would fall apart because you wouldn't be good at thinking on your feet. If you got up an hour late, you would arrive at work an hour late because you would have only one speed, and the call to "Hurry!" wouldn't make you go faster.

The inability to sustain attention or make adjustments and transitions causes many careless mistakes and embarrassing moments. Students with underactive attention and focusing need help learning how to get mental control so they can efficiently take in information, sustain attention, and refocus themselves as they multitask or move from one activity or situation to another. They need to learn to adjust their mental lens so they can zoom in and out with purpose.

The lack of purposeful action keeps these students confused about why they work hard and yet don't get their work done. They sometimes have energy surges that make them hypersensitive to some things and insensitive to others. They often overreact because they have a tendency to pay attention to everything and go off on tangents. At other times, they seem oblivious to both the big picture and the details.

These students may experience confusion about why they don't fit in and can't make friends. Their lack of attention to detail, feelings, and social cues can make them unaware of things they do that others find annoying. Chapter 5 expands on ways we can maximize the potential of the executive brain to flex and pay attention in order to make daily life less stressful. This chapter specifically looks at these interventions in relation to the process of reading.

When focus, attention, and mental flexibility are problems, another executive skill is typically affected—the ability to manage impulses.

Impulse Control

Blake seems to have limitless energy. He is always in a hurry to finish what he is doing. He generally leaves gaping holes in his work because he tears through assignments and checks nothing. Dad refers to him as his "squirrel on steroids" because he jumps from idea to idea or activity to activity. Blake doesn't mean to be offensive when he blurts out unthinking comments; he just doesn't stop to think about how his words might affect others. He is genuinely contrite after hurting someone's feelings but will turn around and do the same type of thing the next day. He seems to be stirring the pot or yanking

someone's chain all the time. When he is not annoying them, the other students find
Blake extremely entertaining, but the teachers don't appreciate his lively behavior.

Now imagine that you are an adult version of Blake. You mean well but say things in a way that you later wish you could take back. You are tempted to fire off a "reply all" e-mail when someone makes you angry. People describe you as being insensitive, hotheaded, or a bull in a china shop. You overcommit yourself in an effort to be helpful but often cannot meet these obligations. Road rage may not be an unfamiliar feeling as you drive, and you have a hard time calming yourself down once you are upset. You buy things you know will lead to financial chaos or have a tendency to jump into situations where angels fear to tread. Priorities like being healthy and spending quality time with friends and family are jeopardized by your inability to control impulses like breaking golf clubs, binge eating, compulsively cleaning, or playing video games. You change plans at the drop of a hat without considering the impact on others.

When dealing with students who have impulse control issues, it is hard to remember that these behaviors are not intentionally uncaring or reckless. Students with this executive delay don't know how to keep their responses proportional to the issue at hand. The emotional part of their brain hijacks their thinking brain, which results in their either overreacting or underreacting to a situation without stopping to consider consequences. A small disappointment can result in hysterics or a complete shutdown when a calm discussion could have solved the problem. "Do now, think later" is the normal mode of operation.

In Chapter 6, I explore interventions that encourage students to slow down and think before they act and that support them in becoming more sensitive to social cues. These strategies will not only help students manage their behavior but also help teachers with classroom management.

Lack of awareness of your own growth or the effect you have on others is a huge barrier to success. If we want to improve in any skill, we have to be able to reflect on whether our efforts are paying off or making things worse. Self-monitoring is the one executive function that has a direct effect on all the other executive skills.

Self-Monitoring

Marlene is a bright student with a remarkable memory. When the teacher asks a
question, she shouts out the answer before anyone else has a chance to think about

it. This makes Marlene feel smart, but today she overheard some girls say she was a showoff. Marlene burst into tears to think that people would accuse her of that.

Let's make your self-monitoring skills as weak as Marlene's. You now have difficulty seeing yourself as others see you. People say you are insensitive because you do things like monopolize conversations and stand too close or talk too loudly for other people's comfort. You blame others when you are unable to reach your goals. You think your low evaluation at work is about the boss not liking you or because your coworkers are not team players. It doesn't occur to you that your work is substandard. You feel helpless because you cannot imagine what you could do to change your situation.

Operating with poor self-monitoring skill is like trying to take care of a 2-year-old while wearing a blindfold. You have a vague sense of where she is and what she needs, but you can do little more than react to situations once they happen. You can't see trouble coming as the toddler tries to pour a glass of milk or stands too close to the top of the stairs.

There is often a sense of hopelessness for students with self-monitoring problems. Because they are unable to accurately evaluate the quality of their work, they cannot see any way to improve their performance. Students who lack insight into how other people think cannot imagine why their peers choose to avoid them or pick on them. They don't ask for help when they need it because they can't identify what they need. The feeling that they are powerless to change things leads to a loss of motivation to keep trying and thus becomes a self-fulfilling prophesy.

For these students, learning how to accurately assess their own performance and use this information to make adjustments goes a long way toward building all the executive skills. In each of the following chapters, we will look at ways to teach students to self-monitor by charting and analyzing their own actions and results so they can figure out the best ways of reaching their goals.

Summary

The executive brain, which does not fully develop until the early to mid-20s, affects the way students concentrate, organize, feel, solve problems, relate to others, and process information. Understanding how executive function develops and what subskills it encompasses helps explain why so many students have difficulty getting work completed and handed in on time, or why they struggle with relationships and self-control.

Lack of skill and coordination of executive brain processes is a good predictor of both academic and behavioral problems. It is crucial for parents and teachers to be aware that many students with delays won't pick up on these skills for a long time, even when shown repeatedly how to handle them. Patience, redirection, and positive feedback are the keys to both academic and behavioral success. We can make a difference, but it will be a marathon, not a sprint.

When adults take this new neurological information into account, they can make more informed decisions about whether children are in an "I can't" or "I won't" mode. It is easier to decide to respond with helpful interventions instead of punishments when educators and families view problems like lack of attention, poor planning, forgetfulness, and impulsiveness as thinking malfunctions rather than attitude or character flaws. This new lens on problem behaviors helps us see the wisdom of providing support rather than simply smacking a label like ADD, oppositional defiant, or lazy on a student.

Identifying underlying reasons for why students respond the way they do is helpful in the development of viable plans of support. This deeper view of student difficulties is the mission of this book and will be modeled and demonstrated in the chapters that follow.

The next chapter takes a more detailed look at some specific planning and problem-solving symptoms that students with executive functioning delays experience and examines how these problems affect both social studies and social performance.

PLANNING AND PROBLEM SOLVING: FAILURE TO LAUNCH AND FOLLOW THROUGH

Faith has talked for two weeks about joining the high school student congress. She truly wants to join the group but has yet to get the packet of information about how to become a member from the social studies teacher. Her mom reminds her each day as she walks out the door, only to have Faith bark out, "I'm doing it! Stop bugging me!"

Shawn likes 4th grade but is having a hard time adjusting to the heavier workload. He has a social studies report due in five days that his teacher, Mrs. Warren, assigned at the beginning of last week. She has asked him for his outline twice, and both times Shawn told her he left it at home. The truth of the matter is, he hasn't even decided on a topic.

First grader José loves that he has finally learned to read. During class time, he readily does his worksheets and volunteers to read aloud in group; however, at home he is not so eager. When it comes to doing his homework, José is an unwilling participant. He dreads homework time because it always seems like it goes on for hours, even though the actual work would only take about 15 minutes if he would stop whining and stalling.

What do these students have in common? Failure to develop and launch a plan of action. Many adults would peg the cause for this failure on procrastination or laziness, but is it laziness or something else? What we are often dealing with in the cases of students like Faith, Shawn, and José is not laziness but an underdeveloped set of executive skills for planning and problem solving. It is not uncommon for adults who work with students who have this type of executive delay to become frustrated and label these students as unmotivated or unwilling. The adults may resort to blaming and lectures, but these labels and "kicks in the pants" only make the problem worse. The real issue isn't that these students *won't* take action but that they *can't.*

Executive dysfunction that looks like lack of motivation is often exacerbated when a student perceives the situation as threatening or blaming (Willis, 2010a). Instead of lecturing or punishing students for poor planning and problem solving, we need to search beneath the surface behavior or attitude for deeper causes for the stalled action. Then we must intentionally and consistently teach the missing initiation and follow-through skills.

Root Causes of Poor Planning and Problem Solving

Determining the root causes of problems is critical to helping the student. The more precise the diagnosis, the better the chances of providing the most effective support. Figure 2.1 (p. 22) is a flowchart to help you analyze typical root causes of delayed executive function in the area of planning and problem solving so that you can choose the best plan of action. In this figure, the primary area of concern appears at the top of the chart and is followed by a listing of subskills to consider. By no means is this a list of all possibilities, but it is a representative sample of typical causes.

As I mentioned in the Introduction, I have found that the most useful way of getting at root causes is to use the "Five Whys" method. This process was developed by Toyota to diagnose problems and find solutions. Its fundamental premise is that it takes at least five iterations of asking "Why?" to get to a root cause. The method is most effective when used by a team of at least two people, one to take the role of questioner or coach and the other to act as the responder. The problem-solving coach asks a series of questions that leads the responder, most often a teacher, to delve into the student's thinking and motivation concerning the problem. A possible question series might look like this:

- Why do you think the student does that?
- What would cause the student to think that way?

2.1 | Root Causes of Poor Planning and Problem-Solving Skills

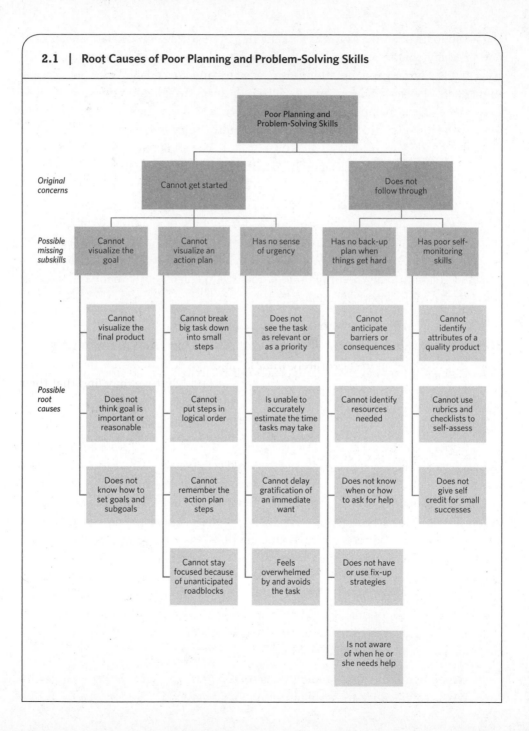

- What skills do you think the student lacks that other students the same age understand and use?
- What is keeping the student from learning these skills?
- What should we concentrate on first?

Instead of focusing on the symptoms, coaching conversations attempt to get into the student's head to analyze the root causes.

The more familiar teachers are with what researchers have discovered to be common causes for problems, the more easily they can answer these questions without going out of their "circle of influence." Our circle of influence is any problem or circumstance over which we have some control. Issues like the need for medication, poor support from home, learning disabilities, and dysfunctional families definitely affect students and can make teaching harder, but teachers usually have little control over them. If we cannot control the issue, it is fruitless to waste time having a conversation about it during the analysis talk, even though it is contributing to the problem.

Let's take a closer look at the problems of our students Faith, Shawn, and José, using this questioning method in combination with the root causes chart to see if we can pinpoint more accurately what is holding each student back. We know they all find it hard to get started on the task at hand, but we may find that their reasons for not moving forward are somewhat different.

Faith

Faith's "laziness" issue has less to do with her unwillingness to get started than with her inability to figure out how to approach problems, especially ones she finds scary, boring, or difficult. Her executive brain has a tendency to freeze when faced with taking the initiative, like approaching a social studies teacher for information or asking for help in math class. The analysis conversation between Faith's teacher and the problem-solving coach might sound like this:

Coach: You said Faith constantly procrastinates. Why do you think she does that?

Teacher: She's just lazy. Once she gets started, she's usually fine, so it isn't about the work being too hard.

Coach: What could be going through Faith's head that makes her choose not to start working?

Teacher: I don't know. Some students want attention, but that doesn't exactly sound like Faith. What else could it be?

Coach [looking at the root causes chart]: Let me throw out a few possibilities. Some students don't start because they feel overwhelmed. They can't get a clear picture of what the finished product should look like even when the teacher explains the task clearly. Occasionally, students have difficulty estimating how much time a task will take. They don't get going because they think they have plenty of time, or they procrastinate because they think the work will take forever. Do any of these things sound like Faith's root cause?

Teacher: Faith understands the assignments. I think it's her lack of motivation more than anything.

Coach: Could there be some missing skills that keep her from being motivated?

Teacher: Well, she can visualize the end product, but I'm not so sure she sees how to overcome obstacles along the way. When things look hard, her tendency is to get upset and then shut down.

Coach: What causes her to shut down?

Teacher: I think she may see asking for help as a sign of weakness, so when faced with a problem she can't solve she just quits.

As the conversation progresses, the teacher develops the hypothesis that Faith stalls out because she has limited success with predicting barriers and making adjustments when plans don't work out. She also has trouble using positive self-talk to get past her mental anxiety. These failure-to-launch problems have a different set of root causes than those Shawn faces.

Shawn

Shawn, who appears to be a procrastinator, is extremely smart and typically does well in short daily assignments when a lot of writing isn't required. Longer assignments look so overwhelming to him that his brain goes into a complete stall every time he thinks about them. The teacher may as well ask him to construct a bridge as do a social studies report. Shawn doesn't have the planning skills to schedule his work in small, sequential steps over time. Couple this with his ability to entertain himself and others when he should be working, and you have a student in trouble academically and behaviorally. The questioning process between Shawn's teacher and the problem-solving coach might go like this:

Coach: What is it that prevents Shawn from handing in his assignments on time?

Teacher: One problem is that he can think of 99 things to do to delay getting started.

Coach: Why do you think he wants to delay the work?

Teacher: I don't know. He is capable but hates to write, and he's just a hot mess when it comes to staying on task. When he does get started, he works on one thing for a few minutes and then jumps to something else. Then he may forget that he didn't finish the first thing he was working on. His mind works like a pinball machine.

Coach: Why do you think he jumps around like that?

Teacher: Part of it is avoidance because he hates paperwork of any kind, and some of the problem is his disorganization and lack of focus.

Coach: What specific skills would help him get organized and focused?

Teacher: He needs to decide on a plan and finish one task before he starts another.

Coach: Why can't he do that now?

Teacher: I'm not certain he knows how to get a good work plan together. He probably doesn't have good self-monitoring skills, either.

This "Five Whys" conversation leads the teacher to see that Shawn's problem is not likely to go away unless she models planning strategies and helps Shawn practice these new techniques until they feel like second nature to him. Our third student, José, has similar problems but with a different emphasis, as we'll see his teacher discover.

José

On the surface, José seems to be an avoider like Shawn. When his teacher asks him to stop working at the science center so he can get ready for math, José says OK but continues to explore the rocks, bugs, and science books he loves. When his mother says it is time to do homework, he promises that he will start as soon as his TV show ends, but he seldom remembers his well-intentioned promise because his executive brain constantly misjudges or loses track of time. José also has trouble switching his focus, especially for attacking work he doesn't enjoy.

During the "Five Whys" interview, the coach asks José's teacher, Mr. Lewis, "Why can't José stop one activity and start another as smoothly as his peers?" At first, the teacher says that José is being defiant. Then the coach asks, "What problem-solving skills might be missing?" Mr. Lewis responds that José can't set priorities and has difficulty stopping one activity to begin another. The coach then asks, "Why is it that José can switch from reading assignments to the science station without much trouble but generally cannot go from station work to getting ready for math class?" Mr. Lewis starts to see that delaying gratification for fun and keeping track of time are other areas where José also needs help.

When "Five Whys" questioning leads to identification of specific skill deficits, the intervention possibilities become much clearer. When difficulties are seen as attitude problems, the most common adult response is to deal out some type of punishment, which results in students finding themselves in hot water when what they really need is guidance in developing problem-solving skills.

Interventions That Help with Planning and Problem Solving

After analyzing root causes of a student's stalled performance, the next step is planning what action you, other school staff, the student, and the student's family will take to help the student progress. In this section, I offer intervention options to address some of the specific root causes, but just as the flowchart of causes is not exhaustive, the intervention options given here are a sampling of possible ways to support students as they cope with delayed executive function in problem solving and planning.

Visualizing Clear Goals

Anxiety about getting started often stems from not having a clear vision of the end product or what steps to take to get there. Having unanswered questions like "Am I going to be able to do this?" or "What is this supposed to look like when I am finished?" is a common roadblock to positive thinking. On the other hand, if you can imagine yourself holding a finished product and feeling the satisfaction of doing quality work, you create a powerful incentive to begin.

All successful people start by creating a picture in their heads of the goal or target they want to reach. Football players see themselves running across the goal line. Dancers see themselves performing perfect moves to the music. Kids and parents see themselves having fun with their friends or checking off jobs on their "to do" list. Being successful at school works the same way.

Let's use Faith's social studies dilemma as an example. Faith really wants to participate in the student congress taking place at her high school, but she understands how challenging this competition is and is afraid she will not be chosen as one of the final delegates. To help Faith generate the courage and motivation to try, she needs to be able to visualize herself going through the steps of applying and succeeding. If I am Faith's teacher, Faith and I begin by making a list of things she needs to do to make her dream actually happen. Then I need to help Faith picture herself being selected and doing the work as her classmates and family cheer her on. She would visualize how proud she would feel as she opened with an engaging attention grabber or as she delivered her arguments by clearly supporting her positions. We would also discuss the feeling of accomplishment knowing that she had stretched herself by giving it her best shot regardless of whether she was selected for the final team or not. This is the secret of champions.

Staying Focused by Anticipating Roadblocks

When assignments don't go as planned, students often stop in their tracks. Stress builds if students think they will be blamed or criticized for work that goes wrong, and they may decide that hiding the problem is better than asking for help. Anticipating roadblocks in advance and talking about ways to overcome them serve as an ounce of prevention (Zins, Weissberg, Wang, & Walberg, 2004). One way of starting this conversation is to focus on someone else's problem that mirrors the same issues the student is likely to face. Because this approach minimizes feelings of threat, it enables a student to think through a back-up plan without becoming defensive or discouraged. A conversation with Faith about anticipating roadblocks might sound something like this:

> Faith, let's imagine we are watching your friend Jake tackle the problem of trying out for the student congress. What would happen if he decided to wait until next week to ask for an application? OK. What would happen if he didn't ask anyone to check his application, and he found out he omitted an important piece of information? What if he waited until the week before tryouts to write and submit his legislation and arguments? Why would he decide to do that instead of getting started? Got it. Can you think of other traps that might prevent Jake from earning his position on the team? Right, if he doesn't have the courage to ask for help when he gets stuck, then he will stay stuck. What choices can he make? We know what kind of mess he can't afford to get into, right? So what kind of things will your friend Jake need to think about so he can put a plan together that gets the job done and relieves some of his stress? Right. How much of Jake's plan will work for you?

In this talk, I raised another issue that can stop a well-laid plan in its tracks. What if the student gets stuck and doesn't ask for help?

Knowing When and How to Access Resources

Many students don't know what to do when they don't know what to do. Being able to identify resources that can help when they get stuck relieves stress and keeps students moving forward. Before Faith starts work, I will ask her two questions: "What will you do if you find you need help on this project?" and "Who and what should we put on a list of people and resources you might need?" The list might include people's names, study group opportunities, a timer, reference books, websites—whatever might support the work.

Some students are able to identify their resources but will need to practice how to approach people on their list. Role-playing is often the best way to get past this barrier. Here is how I might set up role-playing with Faith:

> Faith, I'll be the student, and you be Mrs. Brown for a minute. Help me figure out ways to solve my own problems.
>
> Let's say I don't remember all of the rules for the debate or presentations. How would I start a conversation with Mrs. Brown to let her know I need help? OK, let's try out that conversation by role-playing.
>
> Now I am embarrassed that I don't know what to do in class, but I don't want to ask Mrs. Brown for help. Tell me what I could say to myself so I don't chicken out and just sit here? How does Mrs. Brown respond?
>
> OK, this time I am a student who thinks the teacher is going too fast, and Jerry had my pencil during part of the lesson, so I missed some of the notes. How should I talk to myself about the reason why I don't have the notes? What should I say to Mrs. Brown then?
>
> This time, Mrs. Brown is busy with another student, so I decide just to give up on asking for help because she got upset the last time I interrupted her. What would be some good choices for solving this problem?

Faith and students like her need to understand that asking for help can be hard for anyone. Our job is to help them see that no one wants to appear stupid in front of other people, but not asking for help when it's really needed is not a smart move and leads to more problems. Make the point that getting help is part of being a responsible and successful person. Sometimes emotions and not knowing how to approach someone for help are the core causes of a student's reluctance to approach teachers, and sometimes the reason is the classroom environment.

Relationships and the culture of a classroom can be either an encouragement or a deterrent to students seeking needed assistance. If the teacher scowls and lectures kids who ask for help about the importance of listening the first time, they learn to back off. If students are allowed to make fun of peers who get things wrong or ask questions, the teacher won't get participation or questions from kids who struggle. However, teachers who praise students for being brave enough to ask questions and who set up systems for classmates to help one another solve problems are teaching collaboration skills, independence, and responsibility.

Visualizing Specific Steps of the Action Plan

Each of our example students needs help visualizing not only what his or her end product should look like but also what sequence of steps will get him or her there. Guiding students through a process for solving their own problems is critical to teaching them to be independent. Let's consider Shawn's trouble getting started with his social studies paper. I might start guiding him to problem-solve like this:

> Shawn, I get it when you say you just can't figure out how to get started
> on this big project. Every time I think of cleaning my attic, I suddenly want
> to take a nap or read a book instead. Everyone has those feelings at first
> when a job looks too big to tackle, but let's use a few tricks to make this job
> more manageable. We'll start by listing all the important steps for doing this
> "heroes of the frontier" report, and then we will plan to do one or two parts
> at a time so you still have time for fun.

With some help, Shawn should be able to come up with the steps for preparing the report. That might seem like enough, but many students also require help sequencing the steps.

Putting Steps in Logical Order

Shawn often starts a job and then jumps from task to task, which usually results in poor task completion. He needs help listing his action steps in a logical order. Setting up a chart, timeline, or calendar for recording small steps is helpful because visualization of the process is key to good implementation. Having specific steps written down in a sensible order, however, doesn't necessarily mean Shawn will know how to do each one. It is helpful to ask him clarifying questions, such as

- What materials will you need for this?
- How long do you think this step will take you?
- How do you plan to get started?
- In what order will you do these things?
- What will you do if you get stuck and don't know what to do?

Verbalizing the plan's details provides a mental rehearsal. Initially, Shawn may need someone to work beside him on the same task in order to internalize and reinforce the problem-solving steps. Providing the correct level of support reduces stress and leads to success. Figures 2.2 and 2.3 are examples of a school chart and a home planning chart that can help Shawn learn to plan and execute his work.

Occasionally students become overwhelmed when they see all the steps of a plan at once, so you may have to cover up parts of the calendar or list. Because students' executive skills of problem solving are still developing, it is important to adjust the amount of scaffolding or support you provide. Too much support is as harmful as too little. Start with plenty of modeling and corrective feedback, and then fade the adult support as soon as the students demonstrate the ability to put their own goals into action. The ultimate goal is to enable the students to become more confident and independent; "Support, don't enable" is the motto.

2.2 | Planning Checklist for Social Studies Paper

Steps	What order?	How long?	What materials?
Brainstorm interesting topics	Today	3 min.	
Find two articles on the selected topic	Today	15 min.	Journals in media center
Read articles and take notes	Tomorrow	30 min.	Note cards or computer
Decide what other pieces of information I need and where I can find them	Tomorrow	5 min.	Teacher and media specialist help on this
Start my outline	Thursday	30 min.	Get my graphic organizer

2.3 | Planning Checklist for Cleaning Room

Steps	What order?	How long?	What materials?
Gather all dishes, food, and trash and take them to the kitchen	1	10 min.	Trash bag
Put clean clothes on hangers or shelves	2	5 min.	Hangers
Put dirty clothing in the laundry basket	3	2 min.	Laundry basket
Find a home for anything still on the floor that shouldn't be there	4	10 min.	
Sweep	5	5 min.	Sweeper

Accurately Estimating Time

Like most students his age, José has a hard time visualizing and judging time. He can't get his head around when 10 minutes or half an hour is up. It is the awareness of a deadline that helps people feel a sense of urgency to get started. Teachers and parents need to provide support in this area. Giving students an analogy, like "This will take you about the same amount of time as it takes you to walk to Tom's house or to eat lunch" can help make the concept of time concrete. Once students get the idea of relating minutes to time frames they are familiar with, you can ask them to come up with their own analogies.

Poor pacing also contributes to problems with time management. Students often underestimate how long it will take to do each part of a task. For example, José might plead to wait until after his TV show to start his homework or chores with the full belief that he can get everything accomplished. Helping him put estimated times to each step and setting a timer to see how close his estimates are to reality will serve as good feedback for future planning.

Delaying Gratification

José has difficulty making transitions partly because he can't put fun on hold and get to work. Addressing both the task and the student's emotional objective for fun is important when setting goals. To stay focused on the goal, students need to see that there will be a balance between work and fun. It is normal for children and adults to want to play before work. Children often try to convince you that there will be plenty of time to work after play, but this can be a bad habit to foster.

For beginning goal setters, it is wise to start with tasks that are concrete and challenging but doable within a short time—within the class period for early elementary students or within a day or two for older students. Some good beginning questions to ask the student include

- What do you need to accomplish?
- When will you have this completed?
- What steps do you need to do right now, and what can wait until tomorrow or later?

With these answered, the student can set a clear goal for the work. A goal might sound like this: "I will start my homework before the timer goes off, and I can finish by 7:00," "I will write down three key ideas for my report in the next five minutes," or "I will submit my application in two days."

We now have covered forming a solid plan with the goal, steps, time, and materials visualized, and some back-up ideas for addressing barriers. The skill that will keep a student's plan in motion is self-monitoring.

Building Self-Monitoring Skills

Self-monitoring is the ability to observe and record our own growth and behavior and use those data to make the adjustments that will improve results. This skill builds responsibility and independence. It gives us control over our own thinking by acting as our error-detection and fix-up system. Self-monitoring is effective in developing more appropriate behaviors, like increasing on-task behavior in the classroom, boosting completion of homework assignments, improving both academic performance and social skills, and reducing disruptive behavior (Hallahan & Kauffman, 2000). Five-year-olds start to develop the skill to reflect, but it steadily becomes more sophisticated given good modeling, direct teaching, and practice (Veenman, Wilhelm, & Beishuizen, 2004). Here are a few favorite self-monitoring techniques to use with interventions.

CHECKLISTS AND RUBRICS. Checklists and rubrics are important tools for students who struggle with goal setting. They help students visualize not only the end product and the steps to accomplishing that goal, but also the issues they need to consider for judging quality along the way. Providing in-class modeling and practice in how to use age-appropriate rubrics to score model papers, projects, or filmed performances is powerful. The more students practice matching their own evaluations to the teacher's scoring, the more likely they are to produce quality work, assuming they possess the skills to do the work. This matching process makes the criteria for quality very clear.

My son and I often went to war over whether he had "cleaned" his room. Although he claimed he had cleaned, I saw very little evidence of it. The problem wasn't that he hadn't done any cleaning. The problem was our different visualizations of what the finished product should look like. Once we agreed on a clear list of what constituted "clean," a great part of the problem was solved. I did have to start slowly with only two requirements—nothing on the floor and only seven things on the dresser. Figure 2.4 is our first cleaning rubric. The next week, I saw that we needed to add "no clothes on the bed or chairs." By working together, a specific visual list emerged that resulted in a satisfactory compromise between us.

SELF-EVALUATING AND CELEBRATING SMALL SUCCESSES. Conversations that regularly celebrate small steps that go well and reflect on ways to adjust what isn't working develop executive function skills. Students need lots of modeling and verbal interactions in order to learn the strategy of self-talk that enables people to monitor and adjust their plans. A conversation modeling this kind of self-evaluation for Shawn might sound like this:

> So as you look at your planning checklist, what parts of your plan to
> get this social studies report finished are on target? Good, the first two
> steps are completed. Feels good to say that, doesn't it? That question
> about whether the pioneers were really heroes or villains will really catch
> attention. Is the timing working out the way you thought it would? That's

2.4 | Work Plan Rubric Example

	Perfect	One thing was overlooked	Several things need to be taken care of
Nothing on the floor that does not belong on the floor	✓		
Only seven things can be on the dresser			✓

OK. People often underestimate the time needed for a new task. Don't let that stress you out. Just make sure you adjust and keep going. The estimate doesn't have to be spot-on the first time. How will you use what you learned to help you make a closer estimate next time? Great. Do you want to adjust some of your time estimates for the next two steps, or will your plan still work? The difference between successful and unsuccessful people is not how many mistakes they make; it's how well they learn from their mistakes. You are right on target for learning how to plan your work and estimate your time, and that will help you in all your classes. What, other than adjusting time estimates, will you keep doing to meet your goal? Anything else you want to change to make your plan work even better?

Recognizing patterns of thinking and behaving that work well and seeing their own growth both serve to fuel students' future achievement. Having a list of small tasks written down gives a student the reward of having something to check off. Comparing time estimates with the reality of how long something actually takes helps the brain become more aware of both timing and pacing.

Building step-by-step plans and anticipating tough issues are essential for students with executive function delays. Remember, they will need ongoing guidance and corrective feedback for a long time as these skills develop.

Five-Step Problem-Solving Case Study: Poor Planning and Problem Solving

Now that we have explored root causes of failing to formulate and launch a plan and possible interventions, let's take a look at the whole five-step problem-solving process (Searle, 2007). The steps of this protocol will take you all the way from first spotting a problem to choosing an action plan to solve it. Although we'll be focusing on one case study student, Sara, the five steps can be used for any student, at any grade level, for any academic or behavioral problem. Let's meet our student and teacher and begin.

Sara is in social studies class and has had four reminders to start her assignment. Each time her teacher, Mrs. James, walks by, Sara is either reading her novel or doodling. When Mrs. James asks Sara why she is not doing the assignment, Sara sighs and gets out her paper. When the teacher leaves her desk, Sara just stares at the paper. No writing gets done.

Step 1. Know the Student

Mrs. James is frustrated by Sara's behavior. She repeatedly has this problem with her. She decides to meet with the problem-solving coach about Sara's failure to respond in class. Mrs. James and the coach start by identifying Sara's strengths and areas of concern and listing them in a table (Figure 2.5). This step gives them a balanced picture of the student to start from and helps the teacher to spot connections. The table will also be useful in building an action plan for Sara and will provide a baseline for measuring her progress.

Step 2. Analyze the Root Causes

Focusing on the behavior of most concern, Mrs. James and the coach begin their root cause analysis. As they talk, they use the iterative "Five Whys" questioning method and their knowledge of the subsets of causes to help get closer to what is really going on in Sara's head. The coach is careful to keep the conversation

---

2.5 | Strengths and Concerns Chart for Sara

Name: Sara Torres
Grade: 10

Academic concerns:	Behavior concerns:
• Poor writing fluency • Weak in math problem solving • Cannot answer extended-response questions • Getting an *F* in social studies	• Procrastinates on assignments • Does not complete 45 percent of her assignments • Gives the teacher attitude when corrected • Has defeatist attitude (says that no one in her family writes well or likes social studies)
Strengths to build on:	
• Good reader • Likes reading and drawing • Has several good friends • Relates well to most people • Talented in art	• Attendance is regular • Seems to be paying attention in class and answers questions when asked • Can add and subtract accurately (but is slow at it) • Fluent in math computation

focused on areas within their circle of influence and avoids trying to solve the problems before they know what the root causes are.

Coach: Why do you think Sara just sits there when you ask her to work in social studies class?

Mrs. James: She has this attitude that she doesn't think she can do the work, so there is no sense in trying. Social studies is her least favorite subject.

Coach: What causes that attitude, in your opinion?

Mrs. James: Her family has the same attitude. She says no one in her family likes or is good at social studies.

Coach: That certainly can contribute to the problem, but her family's attitude is out of our control. We do know, however, that not all students whose families have negative attitudes toward a subject react like Sara does. What are some other things that happen in class that might exacerbate this problem of poor attitude?

Mrs. James: I can think of two things. She is slow as a snail with written work, and she consistently gets low grades because she piddles around and doesn't finish her assignments.

Coach: We can talk about her problem with writing skills next, but let's start with analyzing why she doesn't get to work and finish her assignments. Why do you think she does that?

Mrs. James: I really don't know.

Coach [referring to Figure 2.1]: Let me list some possibilities for you, and you can select any that fit Sara. Some students cannot focus during instruction, so they really don't know what to do. Others become overwhelmed by what they are asked to do, especially when they see a big assignment. Some students don't feel a sense of urgency, so they dawdle instead of getting started. Others cannot even visualize a way to get started or a plan to attack the work, so their brain freezes in its tracks. Do any of these seem to fit Sara?

Mrs. James: Sara does focus during class. I don't think that's the issue, but being overwhelmed when she sees writing assignments and feeling no sense of urgency certainly fit her. Let's start there.

Coach: So we need a plan that helps Sara break down big tasks to help her not feel overwhelmed, and we need to have her develop a timed schedule so she feels a sense of urgency. Do you think this will make a difference in her work?

Mrs. James: It's a start. Let's give it a try.

This coach just helped Sara's teacher see Sara's "attitude" problem through the new lens of weak executive functioning, which means Mrs. James will most likely be open to new approaches for solving the problem, especially since she made her own diagnosis.

Step 3. Set a Clear and Measurable Goal

Now that Mrs. James and the coach have identified the root causes of Sara's problem, they can use that information for setting a measurable goal. There are two parts to intervention goal setting. The first is stating a hypothesis that identifies what new tactic the teacher will use to solve the problem and what new outcome is expected from the student as a result. For Sara, Mrs. James and the coach decide on the following:

> **Hypothesis:** If we teach Sara to break down big tasks and to develop her own work schedule, she will complete more assignments on time.

The second part of the goal is the time frame and benchmark that will tell the teacher if the intervention is effective. Mrs. James and the coach arrive at the following for the second part of setting a clear and measurable goal for Sara:

> **Time frame and measurement benchmarks:** Within five weeks, Sara will be able to break down tasks, sequence the steps, and track her own successful completion rate. Sara will go from finishing 45 percent of her social studies assignments to finishing 75 percent on time and earning a minimum grade of *C*.

Step 4. Decide How to Monitor Student Progress

Mrs. James will need data to determine how well Sara is using the new skills and moving toward her goal. The data must specifically show whether Sara is breaking big tasks down into smaller segments and setting estimated time goals and whether these strategies are effective. If these practices are not helping Sara learn to plan her work or develop a sense of urgency to get work done, then the team will revamp its plan. Mrs. James and the coach agree on charting work completed with a minimum grade of *C* as the measurement strategy that will track whether the problem of incomplete work is being solved.

Sara will self-record on the chart, so gathering the data will create very little extra work for Mrs. James. Sara will track three things: how long it took her to get started, how many times she accurately estimated her work time, and how many completed assignments she hands in that result in a grade of *C* or better (see Figure 2.6). All Mrs. James needs to do, other than model the skills, is spot-check Sara's self-monitoring and give her praise and corrective feedback.

Self-charting is actually part of the intervention because a student's use of time typically improves as a result of being more aware of on-task behavior (Hallahan & Kauffman, 2000). When time estimates and actual task times are included, students also improve in their ability to estimate how much time given types of work take as they discuss reasons why their estimates were either accurate or not. Student reflection on the patterns the chart shows and reasons for improvement or lack of it are essential to the process. Don't bother collecting data you don't intend to use for improvement.

The next step in the process is to design the specific action plan that addresses Sara's executive function delays and social studies problem.

2.6 | Sara's Self-Monitoring Chart

Sara's chart for the week of February 6	Monday	Tuesday	Wednesday	Thursday	Friday
I broke down my assignment into chunks	Yes No	Yes No	Yes No	Yes No	Yes No
I started within a minute	Yes No	Yes No	Yes No	Yes No	Yes No
Estimate for completing the first part of the paper/assignment:	___ min.	___ min.	___ min.	___ min.	___ min.
Actual time:	___ min.	___ min.	___ min.	___ min.	___ min.
Estimate for completing the second part of the paper/assignment:	___ min.	___ min.	___ min.	___ min.	___ min.
Actual time:	___ min.	___ min.	___ min.	___ min.	___ min.
Estimate for completing the last part of the paper/assignment:	___ min.	___ min.	___ min.	___ min.	___ min.
Actual time:	___ min.	___ min.	___ min.	___ min.	___ min.
Work completed with a grade of *C* or better	Yes No	Yes No	Yes No	Yes No	Yes No

Step 5. Select an Action Plan from a List of Options

Mrs. James and the coach move on to selecting interventions appropriate for the root causes and goals they have identified for Sara. They choose breaking down tasks, sense of urgency, and visualizing plans as skills to work on. Sara's action plan (see Figure 2.7, p. 40) indicates which strategies are done with the teacher, which are done by Sara herself, and which are done with her parents at home.

To help Sara meet her goal, teachers and parents must give her the proper amount of support. In the beginning, support needs to include repeated modeling followed by the gradual release of adult guidance.

A solid instructional practice uses a "first me, then we, then you" procedure to guide the student through the initial learning process. This approach is commonly known as a *gradual release of responsibility* (Fisher & Frey, 2008).

In the first phase, the adults take on the major workload by modeling rather than explaining the process of breaking a problem down and setting time estimates. At this step, the teacher's thinking needs to be as transparent as possible to the student. Often a process called a "think-aloud" is the most effective way to model the skill to be learned (Lewis, 1982). This technique involves teachers saying aloud whatever they are thinking and feeling as they model the strategy. For Sara, Mrs. James provides the following think-aloud:

> OK, Sara, I am going to pretend that I am a student in this class. I want you to watch me as I decide how to make a plan for completing my social studies assignment. When I am finished, you will take your own paper and use the same thinking I just modeled so you see if this strategy can work for you. We may need to change something here or there to make it fit your own style.
>
> Let's see, on my paper, I have four true-false questions to answer, one extended response, and then a challenge problem at the end of the page. I know I have about 20 minutes to work on this, so I will divide the work into smaller chunks. I like challenge problems better than the true-false or extended response, so I think I will start there. I think I can finish this problem in about five minutes if I get right on it. Maybe I can ask the teacher if I can use a timer to see if I can play "Beat the Clock" on this part. Next, I will do the true-false questions, but I might need a one-minute mental break before I do that. I think those problems will take me about eight minutes. That leaves about seven minutes to do the extended-response question. I think this will work for me because it is easier for me to think of three small

2.7 | Action Plan for Sara

Skills Needed	Teaching Strategies	Student Responsibilities	Suggestions for Parents
Breaking down tasks	• Model the process of deciding how much to do in three minutes. Mark an *X* on the paper where you might take a small break. • Model how to think of big jobs as a set of smaller tasks.	• Break each assignment down into doable pieces or steps before starting and plan mini-breaks between segments. • Discuss with your teacher how you can get back on task after breaks.	• Help Sara break down home chores into mini-tasks.
Sense of urgency	• Model how to set estimates for time needed to do a task.	• Estimate your work segments and check those estimates against the actual time the work takes. • Explain to your teacher how you might adjust your estimates or work habits to make the estimates and actual times match.	• Make estimates and set a timer to see if Sara can complete chores in the time she sets for herself.
Visualizing plans	• Model how to create a visual checklist for the steps needed to complete work. Include scheduled mini-breaks. • Brainstorm a list of mini-break choices (stand and stretch, get a drink, etc.). • Help Sara create a chart or graph to monitor her progress.	• Create your own checklists and work plan. • Update your list of mini-break choices and check with your teacher or parent to see if they are appropriate. • Chart your progress and present your findings to your teacher with plans for how you intend to keep improving.	• Create checklists that describe the steps for things like taking out trash, brushing the dog, and straightening her room, so she knows what the job entails and can visually check the steps off when they are completed. • Show Sara ways you use lists and charts to do your daily work (grocery lists, checkbooks, etc.).

chunks of work rather than one big paper. It will be fun to see if I guessed right on how long each part will take, especially since I am only playing the game with myself and there is no penalty for being wrong. I like that.

In the second step of gradual release, the teacher does less of the work, and the student attempts to use the modeled strategy with some teacher guidance. Mrs. James tells Sara it is her turn: "All right, now you show me how you can use what you just saw me do. You may make different choices for breaking your work down, but try to use the same kind of thinking. I will help you if you get stuck."

Once Sara seems comfortable, after repeated practice using this strategy with teacher support, she needs opportunities to practice with a peer who is working on this same skill. Only when peer work looks stable will the teacher move to the last level and expect Sara to apply the skill independently.

This think-aloud technique can be used in any content area (see specific examples for math in Chapter 3 and for reading in Chapter 5) and for learning any new skills.

Large-Group Application

The first time I implemented a full-blown intervention plan like the one developed for Sara, I felt a bit of panic at the thought of all the other students in my room who might also need interventions before the end of the year and the extra workload that accommodating them all might entail. It wasn't until the school counselor suggested not thinking in terms of one student at a time that I realized there wasn't a student in any of my classes who wouldn't benefit from some form of guidance in planning and scheduling their work.

I began providing a choice of planning checklists like Sara's to help other students set their own goals and schedules for assignments. Not all students needed ongoing modeling and corrective feedback to carry out these tasks, but several in every class did. I immediately noticed a marked improvement in both the quality and timeliness of the work I received from my students. I also had fewer phone calls from parents begging for extensions.

Another problem-solving strategy that worked beautifully for me was practicing with rubrics before giving students a new type of work. We did whole-class practice applying a rubric to a model paper or project that was similar but not the same as their upcoming assignment. I didn't want them to simply copy the model.

First, the students would independently use the rubric to score a model paper or project on a scale of 1–100. Next, they would compare their results with the scores of a partner and come to consensus on any scores where there was more than a 5-point difference. This resulted in some lively arguments. Sometimes, I would have each pair of students compare results with another pair, which rekindled the debates. Having to justify their scoring pushed students to think through the rubric, not just choose a number. This process was worth every minute of class time spent on it.

Finally, the students would compare their results with the score my teaching team had agreed on. At times, the teachers would reconsider and adjust their own scoring based on issues students raised. Because these discussions were open and not done for a grade, students said they felt safe expressing opinions and ideas. The process clarified for teachers and students alike what constituted quality work and why. The quality of the assignments I received from students improved significantly every time I implemented this process.

Teaching problem solving using careful goal setting, planning, and self-monitoring ended up not only benefiting the students academically and emotionally but also saving me time in the long run. I spent less time chasing down assignments and regrading papers and projects that had to be redone because of missing pieces or poor quality.

Summary

It is normal and natural for students to experience some level of difficulty with problem solving, planning, initiating, and self-monitoring because the part of their brain that controls this type of thinking does not mature until they reach their early to mid-20s. Students with executive dysfunctions often appear to be lazy and unmotivated when they repeatedly fail to complete and hand in assignments, but the problem is often as much an "I can't" as an "I won't" issue. Adults must have tons of patience and provide lots of modeling, practice, and encouragement to support the development of good planning and problem-solving skills.

WHAT WORKS: Helping students set clear goals and visualizing action plans with small steps and detailed timelines; anticipating trouble spots before they happen and developing a back-up plan; identifying resources and ways to access them; using checklists, rubrics, and self-questioning to reflect on actions; replaying experiences and analyzing why things happened the way they did; providing direct feedback and checking it with their perceptions.

WHAT DOESN'T WORK: Challenging students' excuses for actions rather than redirecting their efforts; assuming they are repeating mistakes to be obstinate or lazy; assigning work that is too difficult for their skill level or work that is not challenging enough; waiting too long to provide corrective feedback; not providing modeling followed by opportunities to recover from mistakes; doing planning *for* them rather than *with* them.

Adults who can keep student brain development issues in perspective will have an easier time being supportive and patient, especially with students whose executive control functions lag behind those of their peers.

On Your Own

Try out the five-step problem-solving process using one of the following case studies. Remember to (1) know the student, (2) analyze the root causes, (3) set a clear and measurable goal, (4) decide how to monitor student progress, and (5) select an action plan from a list of options that involves home, school, and the student working together. (Keep in mind that blank forms for each step can be downloaded at www.ascd.org/ASCD/pdf/books/searlefivesteps2013.pdf. Unlock the PDF using the password "searle113019.")

> *Case study 1.* On Tuesday, Benson's study hall teacher asks why he is sleeping when he knows he has studying to do. Benson assures her that nothing is due until Friday so he doesn't have anything to do today. Last week it was the same story, and he ended up in a panic Thursday night trying to slap together his science paper, due Friday morning.
>
> *Case study 2.* Jimmy likes to linger in the block center when his teacher announces that it is time to clean up and come to circle. Even though his teacher reminds him repeatedly to put the materials away, he gets distracted by whatever center he is working in. He also has a hard time sitting still and listening during circle time.
>
> *Case study 3.* Julia sits and stares at her art project even though she normally enjoys this type of work. She knows that when she finishes the project, she has to make a presentation on her techniques to the whole class, and that thought scares her to death.

MEMORY SKILLS:
WHY DO I STINK AT MATH?

Even though Ellie is in the 5th grade, she struggles to pay attention in class. She genuinely wants to do better, especially in math. Memorizing basic math facts has always been hard for her, but finally she can do the math worksheets the teacher assigns, as long as there is no time limit. Thought problems, however, stop her in her tracks. By the time she reads the whole question, she cannot remember what the first part said, so she resorts to her "guess and go" method, which seldom works. The gaps in her understanding of math concepts and her poor attention to detail make the work so overwhelming to Ellie that she feels like giving up.

Tyrone's 1st grade teacher has contacted a coach for help. When she asks her students to get out a pencil and do the first three problems on page seven in the math workbook, Tyrone gets out his book but seldom remembers what he is supposed to do next. He cannot copy even simple things from the board, and all learning seems to break down in math class. For example, every time Tyrone sees a basic addition or subtraction problem, like 7 + 5, he starts counting up from 0, and when he runs out of fingers, his accuracy suffers. Even though his mom practices the flash cards with him every night, they don't seem to be getting anywhere. "Here tonight, gone tomorrow" appears to be a pattern with Tyrone.

Kirk is having the same type of problems in 9th grade as he did in junior high. He seems to understand the math lesson when his teacher asks him questions that day, but by the next day, things are fuzzy. He frequently makes careless mistakes, such as skipping steps when solving complex problems. In fact, he sometimes skips entire rows of problems, especially under testing conditions. If the work is too demanding, he generally gives up instead of asking for help. Kirk's teacher thinks that if Kirk would just slow down and recheck his work before handing it in, he would be able to get rid of the D on his report card. The coach thinks the problems may have more to do with a lack of deep understanding because of an inability to see and remember patterns.

Memory problems can be bewildering to both students and teachers. Students who can't master skills often feel that it's impossible to succeed. They try and try with no improvement. One of my students described his memory problems as feeling like he had a "Teflon brain" because nothing seemed to stick. Teachers and parents are left wondering why no information appears to penetrate or why what is learned seems to evaporate; could it be a learning disability, carelessness, disinterest? In this chapter, I give you some tools for identifying specific memory problems and offer research-based strategies for bridging gaps in this executive function.

Root Causes of Poor Memory

As we saw in Chapter 1, memory is broken down into three types of processes. Students can experience problems with the way they encode, or take in, information to short-term memory; the way they process material in working memory; or the way they store and retrieve information in long-term memory. Although Ellie, Tyrone, and Kirk are all having trouble with math, their problems don't look very similar. This may be because they are having difficulty in different areas of the memory system.

To help you pinpoint a student's specific memory problem, Figure 3.1 (p. 46) describes some of the key barriers experienced in each of the three memory systems. Although it takes time to sift through the student's symptoms, the effort

3.1 | Root Causes of Memory Problems

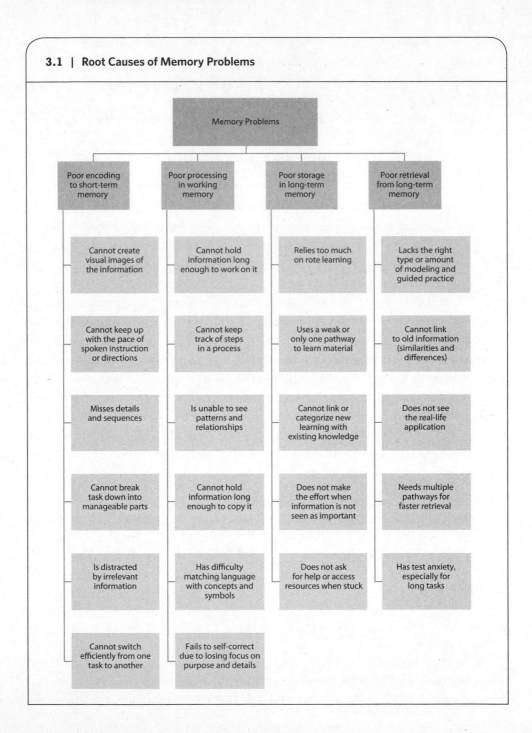

spent in diagnosing root causes means you are more likely to select interventions that yield good results.

As you look over this flowchart, keep Ellie, Tyrone, and Kirk in mind. Which issues do you think might be at the root of their problems?

It looks like Ellie's inattentiveness during instruction may be due to encoding, or intake, problems. The pace and quantity of information delivered can cause a student with a delay in development of this executive skill to feel overwhelmed. As a result, Ellie might overlook details, become distractible, forget instructions, and give up when frustration sets in.

Tyrone has telltale signs of a problem with his working memory: when the teacher has him copy things from the board, he always makes tons of errors. He simply cannot hold the information in his head long enough to get it on paper accurately. Tyrone can't remember what to do when trying to follow multistep instructions that are not routine. He generally remembers the first and last thing he heard, but there is often a muddle with the middle steps. Poor working memory is characterized by inattentiveness, difficulty following instructions, poor organization, and losing track of progress when doing complex tasks.

And for Kirk, our attention should be on building long-term memory skills. Because he seems to know the material one day and lose it the next, addressing storage and retrieval gaps looks promising. Also, we can see that test anxiety may be a long-term memory issue.

Next, we'll look at some options for interventions for memory problems and then tackle identifying specific gaps in our students' math skills.

Interventions That Help with Memory

The following research-based strategies are grouped by the type of memory problem they address.

Encoding

Ellie and other students with encoding problems need interventions that will reduce the cognitive load of incoming information when they are working on difficult material. Here are some effective options (Clark, Nguyen, & Sweller, 2006):

- *Model lessons, assignments, and instructions* in small sequential steps that show the entire process so students can recombine the steps later.

After modeling, have learners do deliberate guided practice with partially completed problems as you give corrective feedback. Gradually decrease the amount of support as students become more comfortable with putting the entire process together for themselves. This technique has an especially powerful effect when used in small-group instruction (three to six students).

- *Start by telling students exactly what to focus on and why.* Students with memory problems tend to miss big ideas and important details, like steps in a process, if their attention is not specifically drawn to them.

- *Have students verbalize and draw images or use concrete techniques and materials* as they learn. This strategy will help link skills and concepts to both the students' verbal and visuospatial memory systems through active learning.

- *Use brain-friendly memory tools* like mnemonics, songs, rhymes, and analogies to help the students capture complicated processes and steps. "Please Excuse My Dear Aunt Sally" is a common mnemonic for helping students remember the order of operations in an equation (Parentheses, Exponents, Multiply, Divide, Add, Subtract). You can find more ideas for memory tools online at www.onlinemathlearning.com/math-mnemonics .html.

- *Teach students to highlight important information* and to make margin notes as they read. These strategies visually separate important from less important facts.

Working Memory

In addition to not being able to hold information long enough to work with it, switching focus is a problem for students with working memory delays. Going from working on math problems to copying down the homework assignment can tax their working memory's capacity. These students are not able to hold as much information in working memory at one time as other students and therefore need more time to process information and refocus themselves.

Analyzing facts, applying rules, remembering the sequence of steps, and following through on directions are all tough working memory challenges. Students with delays in this executive function can't "chunk" information into meaningful units. This inability affects their understanding because they cannot see patterns or see how the new learning connects with things they already know. Rote learning that is not anchored in understanding makes recall much harder, so Tyrone's difficulty with counting needs to be solved by developing his concrete sense of numbers and their patterns.

But there are interventions that will help support these students as they build working memory skills (Levine, 2002):

- *Avoid or reduce the amount of copying required* for students with visual memory weakness, if the purpose of the lesson is not learning to transfer information accurately. Allow these students to write directly on worksheets, highlight in books, or, if copying is necessary, give them plenty of time. For complicated formulas or problems, give students printed copies rather than have them copy from the board or overhead.
- *Use visual aids* like number lines and matrix charts, visual lists of steps, and concrete material to help chunk information into mental images that make relationships and patterns more obvious.
- *Teach the learners to repeat directions* to a partner as well as develop their inner language to repeat and picture steps or directions to themselves. Repeating and seeing things in their minds can be very difficult for students with auditory and visual weaknesses, but don't give up. It works.
- *Use engaging games and activities* to help students practice and apply strategies to unfamiliar situations. This technique promotes flexible thinking. The additional benefit is that enjoyable activities trigger positive feelings, which increase memory functions. (See websites like www.coolmath-games .com for ideas and templates that will make it easy for you or your students to create games.)
- *Create consistent routines for ongoing tasks* like getting materials ready for class, responding in class, or recording homework assignments. When procedures are automatic, working memory capacity is freed for more demanding work.

Long-Term Memory

"Here today, gone tomorrow" is often what teachers experience with students who have delays in long-term memory function. Like Kirk, these students frequently understand the lesson today only to come back tomorrow with a blank stare. If the teacher reteaches the information the same way, the next day the same thing happens: the student is clueless. If Kirk crams when he studies, the information generally does not anchor itself to prior knowledge and therefore does not stick in long-term storage. Now he has both a storage and a retrieval problem. Kirk and other students with these issues need speedy and efficient fact and process retrieval strategies. Let's look at some research-based guidelines to follow when teaching students with these problems.

- *Create multiple storage and retrieval paths* for important concepts by using symbols, antonyms, synonyms, songs, sentences, skits, discussions, examples, or movements that elaborate on the same information. Filing information in several places in the brain (auditory, visuospatial, kinesthetic) makes recall easier and faster. Marzano, Pickering, and Pollock's (2001) research shows that students don't generally achieve 80 percent mastery until they practice a skill at least 24 times.
- *Provide opportunities for repeated practice* to strengthen pathways to information. This strategy is especially effective if the practice is done in a variety of interesting ways to keep students from zoning out from boredom (Holmes et al., 2010).
- *Teach students to revise notes regularly and use visual organizers* to consolidate information into categories for easier mental retrieval and access later (Sadoski & Paivio, 2001).
- *Make sure students can explain why the information or skill is relevant.* Because the brain will not store information not seen as useful or important, helping students see the relevance and application of what is taught is essential. The more personally meaningful the activity and the more directly new information is connected to prior memories, the more efficient the learning.
- *Spend extra time on what is learned in the middle of lessons.* Ask students having long-term memory issues to make up a test for the class or to do an oral review with a partner to ensure they focus on all the parts of the lesson (Wolfe, 2001).

While delays in the executive function of memory affect all learning, students with memory problems seem to have particular trouble with math. In the next section, we will investigate how memory issues specifically affect math achievement.

Root Causes of Persistent Problems in Math

When students have difficulty in math, the problem often traces back to a weakness in their memory systems. Deficits in memory make it hard to recall basic facts, vocabulary, steps in a process, and math rules, and, especially, to remember them while concentrating on all the other aspects of a multistep problem. According to Susan Gathercole (Gathercole, Pickering, Knight, & Stegmann, 2004), poor working memory is a contributing factor for 52 percent of all students who experience ongoing problems in math.

Figure 3.2 (p. 52) is a flowchart to help you identify the specific root causes of problems in math. The four major areas listed on the chart—poor problem-solving skills, poor fluency with basic facts, lack of perseverance, and lack of self-monitoring —are the most typical issues that come up during diagnostic sessions. Remember that both this chart for math problems and the chart showing root causes of memory problems (Figure 3.1) are supposed to be used together with the "Five Whys" questioning method by a team of educators concerned about the student. It is this combination of knowledge of causes and thoughtful probing of the student's problems that yields an accurate diagnosis and effective intervention selection.

While you review the chart, think about Ellie, Tyrone, and Kirk and which skill issues might be at the root of their troubles.

Interventions for Students with Persistent Problems in Math

There are many research-based intervention options that can help students who have problems in math. Here are six intervention categories that research shows yield significant results.

Reading Math Text

Comprehending math text is often tougher than understanding text in other subject areas. Reading math poses unique challenges, which may be what's holding up Ellie each time she tries to solve a word problem. Mathematics text is dense; math writing generally contains more concepts per sentence and paragraph than any other kind of text (Reehm & Long, 1996). Math requires decoding of words, symbols, charts, graphs, and signs. In addition, math often requires students to read vertically, horizontally, and, occasionally, diagonally,

3.2 | Root Causes of Persistent Problems in Math

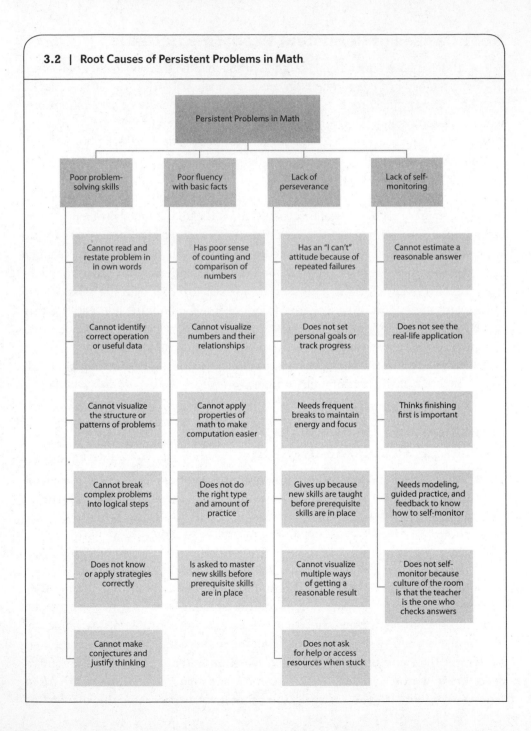

which can be confusing to struggling readers. To add to these difficulties, when reading a word problem, the main idea is frequently at the end of the problem instead of in the topic sentence.

Math has its own vocabulary, and common words can have meanings that are totally different from their meaning in everyday language (e.g., *product, difference, mean, similar, operation, prime, rational, odd*). These dual meanings make reading math extra tricky.

All of these factors can combine to overload students who have memory dysfunction. Here are a few hints for helping students make sense of math texts (Gersten et al., 2009):

- *Have students preview the text* and ask themselves, "What do I need to know when I am finished?" Then, before they figure out the answer to the problem, have them write a declarative sentence with a blank space in it that draws attention to the answer they need to find.

     For example, let's say Ellie's word problem is "Julia has saved $14 so far, but she wants to buy a bracelet that costs $19.99; how much more money does Julia need to save?" Before she starts to work the actual problem, Ellie would write, "Julia needs ____ more to be able to buy her bracelet." Clarifying the problem before working on the solution helps students focus on essential information and correct operations.

- *Have students reread and underline important words* in the passage. Tell them to be careful not to skip important small words, such as *of, all, each, half, and, same,* and *twice.* These words can signal what operation to use (Kenney, Hancewicz, Heuer, Metsisto, & Tuttle, 2005).

- *Ask students to define difficult vocabulary words* and see if their definitions make the text clearer. A great website called the Intermath Dictionary (http://intermath.coe.uga.edu) is very helpful for middle and high school students. This site defines words, gives examples, and provides models of how terms are used in everyday life. It also provides related words, short interactive assessments, and challenge questions.

Visualizing to Develop Number Sense and Memory

Students like Tyrone who have working memory problems often have trouble visualizing information in order to make sense of it. A researched technique known as *CRA* (concrete to representational to abstract) has been shown to be highly effective in building number sense by using precise mental images (Miller & Mercer, 1993). The CRA strategy uses three phases, each building on the one before.

In the *concrete* phase, the teacher talks through and models each step of a process using concrete materials, such as colored blocks, Unifix cubes, tangrams, number frames, algebra tiles, or geometric figures, to help students develop a hands-on form of problem solving. The teacher always uses the appropriate numbers and symbols along with concrete materials to help students recognize how the problem will look when written in the traditional form. To see how this works, let's follow Mr. Marlow as he uses CRA to teach his students, including some with memory function delays.

Mr. Marlow is teaching his students how to add a negative integer and a positive integer. Working with integers tends to be a stumbling point for Mr. Marlow's students every year. This year he wants them to be able to visualize the process. First, he lays out two colors of chips. Yellow chips represent positive integers, and red chips represent negative integers. Mr. Marlow shows students how to come up with the right answer to a problem like $7 + (-9)$ by matching pairs of red and yellow chips. If he has 7 yellow chips and 9 red ones, students can easily see that he has two negative integers left, so the answer is 2. Mr. Marlow starts with easy problems and then will up the ante by giving more complex problems as students become comfortable visualizing the concept.

After watching and listening as the teacher uses manipulatives, students engage in partner practice. Teachers should repeat this first learning phase, or concrete step, of CRA multiple times with many levels of problems until the students can consistently articulate the problem-solving strategy.

When Mr. Marlow is ready to stop using chips, he starts demonstrating a representational method of problem solving using a number line. He will continue to combine writing the abstract form of the problem, $7 + (-9)$, with the representational form as he models.

During this second *representational* phase, the teacher shows students how to solve the same kinds of problems using two-dimensional visuals like sketches, drawings, diagrams, pictures, tallies, or number lines to display and work the problem instead of using concrete manipulatives. The teacher also uses the numerals, words, and symbols to match the visual representations at every step. (You can practice the representational phase of CRA using a bar model at the Singapore Math website: www.singaporemath.com.)

Students then use this slightly more abstract "seeing" step to practice as the teacher provides corrective feedback. When the teacher sees that students can explain the relationship between the math drawings and the symbols, it is safe to go on to the last step.

In the final *abstract* phase of CRA, Mr. Marlow models how he solves problems using only math words, numerals, and symbols. Then it is the students' turn to try. Partnered practice is helpful for students with memory problems because they must focus on all the steps of the process to share their thinking. In the CRA method, it is important to model each step clearly. Using a think-aloud is a powerful way to do this direct instruction.

Using Think-Alouds for Explicit Instruction

When students don't follow the correct steps for math problem solving, the cause may be poor memory for sequences or not having internalized the process well enough to apply it. Students with either issue do better when given specific steps for getting started, a list of small steps for doing the task, and the type of feedback that reduces the anxiety of making errors. Nothing fills this bill like a think-aloud, in which the teacher models and articulates the thinking for carrying out each step and using fix-up strategies (Tournaki, 2003). We'll follow Mrs. Ortega as she uses think-alouds in her classroom to teach the process for solving algebraic word problems.

Mrs. Ortega starts her small-group instruction by modeling a problem-solving strategy using manipulatives and diagrams. As she writes and verbalizes each step of the math process, she creates a poster that outlines her think-aloud steps:

- "Let's see, first I need to figure out what am I trying to solve. That's it. I need to find the value of x to see how much more money John will have than Bill by the end of the month."
- "The most important information is . . ."
- "This information about Sandy isn't important, so I will cross it out."
- "The strategy I think fits this problem best is . . ."
- "First, I will . . ."
- "What should I try next? I am going to . . . Oh, no. I think I forgot a step. I will need to go back and . . ."
- "Now, I will double-check my math."
- "Does this answer make sense?"

Once students have collectively walked through several think-alouds to model the same process, they need to practice the strategy on their own. Mrs. Ortega is careful not to throw students into the deep end of independent practice too soon. First, she has students practice the same strategy with a partner while she listens to see if they can articulate what they are to do.

Vygotsky's (2012) work shows how developing students' "inner voice" helps them learn more efficiently and intentionally. Oral practice with a partner helps students accelerate their ability to identify a problem, develop and execute plans, remember, and self-monitor. This practice works best when partners are taught to ask each other questions that require summarizing, clarifying, and predicting.

Research (Schunk & Cox, 1986) shows that during the early stages of concept development, students do better when they verbalize processes and steps as they work instead of simply working problems silently. This is especially true for students with compromised memory development. The more aware students are of the explicit structure of a process, the better they will be able to verbalize and internalize the information (Meyer, Young, & Bartlett, 1989). Verbalization also gives the teacher valuable information about the quality of student understanding and possible misconceptions.

Without quality feedback, very few strategies make a significant difference in student achievement. Now we will look at some guidelines for effective feedback procedures.

Self-Monitoring Through Corrective Feedback

Research shows that quality feedback consistently improves student learning. The operative word in that statement is "quality," because how feedback is given makes a huge difference in results. Simply marking or telling students that the answer is right or wrong can actually have a negative effect on achievement. Providing the correct answer has a moderate effect. But when teachers tell students *why* the answer is right or wrong, and then ask them to rework the problem correctly, achievement gains are often as much as 20 percentile points (Marzano et al., 2001).

All students, but especially those with memory problems, need guidance discovering ways to self-monitor and fix misconceptions. In the corrective feedback process, when a student makes an error, the teacher immediately models the correct procedure, prompts the student to correct his or her own response, and then follows up by reinforcing the strategy again (Darch, Carnine, & Gersten, 1984). Teaching students to use tools like personalized checklists and rubrics also helps them become more aware of what to look for as they check for their most common errors.

The feedback and self-monitoring process increases motivation and achievement by helping students see that they are learning even when they fail at a task. Students who are encouraged to fix mistakes are also more likely to ask for assistance when they need it.

Continuous review of concepts and procedures is another aspect of increasing student achievement.

Cumulative Review Strategies

Students like Kirk can encode information and seem to understand it immediately after instruction, but have difficulty with the memory storage and retrieval process. Here are a few research-based strategies to help students with long-term memory issues.

- *Short daily cumulative reviews* that combine mastered skills with just a few new skills help reduce the frustrations of learning new material for students experiencing memory problems. For instance, when studying math flash cards, I give struggling students eight cards with known combinations and two cards with unknown facts. Having this 80 percent success rate makes practice more enjoyable and delivers the new material in smaller chunks. Because the percentage of new material provides a challenge without making the goal too difficult, motivation generally remains high (Locke & Latham, 2002). As students become fluent with the new fact cards, I replace two of the well-known cards with two new ones.
- *Quick verbal recaps* are another simple review strategy that makes a big difference in long-term memory storage and retrieval. Asking students to turn to a partner and articulate what they just learned and how it will be useful in the future teaches reflection skills. For example, after the day's math lesson, Mr. Williams asks small groups of students to debrief what they learned about long division. Students talk about what new words they learned, what steps they need to remember, and how they should use the think-aloud chart to guide their word choices and thinking. Mr. Williams might guide the discussion like this: "What can you do now that you could not do last week? Great, and how will that help you in the future?

Can you give me an example? Very good. When would you ever use this strategy if you were not in school?"

This recap is especially helpful for students like Kirk, who have memory barriers because they tend to forget the purpose of the lesson as they try to apply new skills. Verbalization not only reconnects the dots for them but also strengthens mental pathways for later retrieval.

- *Associating difficult concepts with sayings or visualizations* is a third way to link new material to long-term memory. The crazier the word or image, the better it is for memory. This process is sometimes called "pegging." For example, when I want to remember the rules for multiplying negative and positive integers, I just remember a little saying my algebra teacher taught me:

> When good things happen to good people, that is good. $+$☺
> (A positive × a positive = a positive.)
> When good things happen to bad people, that is bad. $-$☹
> (A positive × a negative = a negative.)
> When bad things happen to good people, that is bad. $-$☹
> (A negative × a positive = a negative.)
> When bad things happen to bad people, that is good. $+$☺
> (A negative × a negative = a positive.)

Students who have verbal memory problems often do better with silly or bizarre cartoons, songs, or rhymes than with verbal cues. Visit http://www.buildyourmemory.com/pegging.php for a few more ideas.

The last intervention option we will discuss is basic drill and practice. In this section, it will be important to remember that the adage "Practice makes perfect" only works when you are practicing perfectly. When rote memorization of math facts and concepts comes before understanding, practice wastes more time than it saves and actually interferes with long-term memory. But if you have used the preceding interventions to lay a solid framework first, drill and practice is very effective.

Drill and Practice for Fact Fluency

Students who have number sense, like Kirk and Ellie, benefit from drill and practice to sharpen their skills and fluency. According to research (Gersten et al., 2009), 10 minutes of each math class should be spent building fluid retrieval of basic math facts. This drill and practice should go beyond just the "mad minute" type of computation quizzes. Building fluency by practicing strategies that emphasize number relationships (e.g., number families, doubling patterns, and number line activities) is recommended—for example, problems like "If $4 \times 2 =$ __, what is $40 \times 2 =$ __?" or "If I add negative three to positive two, the answer is____." These types of problems strengthen mental math skills.

Researchers also recommend setting specific, challenging, but achievable goals for student practice. Don't simply say, "Do your best on this paper." Throw out a challenge: "Let's see if you can do the next four problems in eight minutes" (Locke & Latham, 2002). Short sessions using combinations of practice, corrective feedback, and, when necessary, direct instruction with verbalization significantly increase student achievement for learning the basics.

Five-Step Problem-Solving Case Study: Lack of Number Sense and Poor Memory

With our understanding of root causes of memory and math problems and our lists of intervention options for both, we are now armed to tackle a student problem using the five-step protocol. Our struggling student is Marcus.

Marcus is a 2nd grader who seems to be in his own little world a great deal of the time. His teacher, Mrs. Ackerman, is frustrated because when the work gets challenging, Marcus gives up. His defeatist attitude and lack of focus are bound to contribute to an ever-deepening dip in his achievement.

Marcus's mother works hard with him at home, but so far, nothing seems to be helping. Marcus enjoys working with a partner, but he sometimes lets the partner do the work for him. Marcus is much stronger visually than auditorily, which should help him with math, but that doesn't seem to be paying off, either.

Step 1. Know the Student

Mrs. Ackerman is worried about Marcus. He is falling increasingly behind in math, and she doesn't know what else to try. Finally, she decides to enlist the help of a 5th grade teacher who has been trained to be a problem-solving coach. The coach asks Mrs. Ackerman to list her concerns about Marcus's academic progress and behavior. The coach also asks Mrs. Ackerman to think about Marcus's

3.3 | Strengths and Concerns Chart for Marcus

Name: Marcus Townes
Grade: 2

Academic concerns:	Behavior concerns:
• Poor math fact fluency • Weak in math problem solving • Cannot figure out which math operation to use • Weak vocabulary skills	• Daydreams in class • Gives up when work is challenging • Says he is dumb • Often skips problems or even entire rows of problems • Cannot remember directions

Strengths to build on:

• Excellent at drawing
• Outgoing and friendly
• Relates well to most children and adults
• Plays piano well

strengths and list them as well. Figure 3.3 shows what Marcus's strengths and concerns chart looks like when Mrs. Ackerman has finished.

Step 2. Analyze the Root Causes

The coach begins the discussion to analyze for root causes with a "why" question about Marcus's trouble in math and continues probing each of Mrs. Ackerman's replies with another question. Remember that it takes at least five questions to get to a root cause. During the conversation, the coach is careful not to try to solve the problem before the teacher has done the work of probing beneath the surface symptoms for the root causes. Let's take a look at what insights this thoughtful dialogue yields:

Coach: Why do you think Marcus is having such a hard time in math?

Mrs. Ackerman: For one thing, he doesn't pay attention in class. In fact, he doesn't seem to be paying attention when he does his work. He tries at first and then starts skipping problems—sometimes, entire rows of problems.

Coach: What causes that lack of focus?

Mrs. Ackerman: I think he is so confused by math that he just shuts down.

Coach: What parts of math work give him the most trouble?

Mrs. Ackerman: We are working on double-digit subtraction with regrouping, and he doesn't have a clue. He still counts on his fingers, and, of course, that doesn't work now that we are into higher numbers. I gave him counters and a number line, but he won't use them.

Coach: Why won't he use the visual aids?

Mrs. Ackerman: Because there are only seven kids who still use the visuals regularly. I think he is embarrassed to still need manipulatives, but he said the tools mix him up.

Coach: What is it about the tools that mixes him up?

Mrs. Ackerman: When I watch him use a number line, for example, if he is subtracting 5 from 12, he might count the 12 as the first jump rather than the move from 12 to 11. He also forgets what number he just said, or sometimes he counts a number twice. He does the same thing with counters.

Coach: What beginning skills do you think are missing that might cause that problem?

Mrs. Ackerman: Other than his inability to count accurately, I don't know. What do you think?

Coach: I think you are right. The basic visualization of one-to-one correspondence for counting forward and backward seems weak. That may mean that his concept of which number is greater or less could also be faulty. We can assess this skill to see if we are right.

The other thing that occurs to me is that he may be having a hard time holding information in his head long enough to work on it. Blanking out during class, forgetting his place, and having little success remembering math facts all sound like memory problems.

Mrs. Ackerman: Can we do anything about that?

Coach: Fortunately, yes. It might take a longer time for him to make progress than it would if his memory functions were strong, but we can definitely do things that make a difference.

The coach was able to help Mrs. Ackerman uncover some possible missing skills. Notice that Mrs. Ackerman thought Marcus was embarrassed about needing to use manipulatives, but the coach pointed out that Marcus actually reported to the teacher that they mixed him up. Many students with weak working memory choose not to use visual aids when given an option because it stretches their multitasking capacity. Like Marcus, they would rather revert to less helpful strategies, such as counting on their fingers, guessing, or memorizing things they don't understand. None of these strategies works for long, and they can actually impede long-term storage. Before requiring Marcus to use visual aids independently, Mrs. Ackerman may need to model and practice their use in a small group until the process becomes more comfortable (St. Clair-Thompson, Stevens, Hunt, & Bolder, 2010).

Assessments verified that Marcus has an unclear sense of number quantity. He isn't able to visualize and sequence numbers in his head. He can identify the greater number only 40 percent of the time. He counts accurately about 60 percent of the time and makes most of his mistakes between the numbers 11 and 20. This lack of visualization, or number sense, is an encoding problem that keeps Marcus from seeing patterns and relationships among symbols, concrete materials, and words that represent quantities (working memory problem).

Step 3. Set a Clear and Measurable Goal

The next step is to use this diagnostic information to set a short-term, measurable goal. Mrs. Ackerman and the coach formulate a hypothesis that sets out what they plan to do to help Marcus and what the predicted outcome will be.

> **Hypothesis:** If we teach Marcus to visualize how numbers work and teach him memory strategies, he will develop one-to-one correspondence and be able to count accurately.

Next, they estimate a time frame in which they should see improvement in Marcus's skills and fix a measurable goal for quantifying that improvement. They settle on the following:

> **Time frame and measurement benchmarks:** Within four weeks, Marcus will be able to identify which number is greater 90 percent of the time, and he will be able to count forward and backward between 0 and 20 starting at any number, both with and without aids.

Step 4. Decide How to Monitor Student Progress

Once the goal is set, Mrs. Ackerman and the coach focus on specific ways to track Marcus's progress. Mrs. Ackerman develops two ways for Marcus to monitor his own growth. She creates eight greater-and-less-than sheets using only numbers 0 to 20. Each sheet includes the same 20 problems but in different order. Every week, she assesses Marcus's ability to identify the larger and smaller numbers. Figure 3.4 shows the chart that Marcus will use to self-record his progress.

3.4 | Marcus's Self-Monitoring Chart for Greater and Less Than

Number of correct > or < problems						
20						
19						
18						
17						
16						
15						
14						
13						
12						
11						
10						
9						
8						
7						
6						
5						
4						
3						
2						
1						
Week #	1	2	3	4	5	6

Mrs. Ackerman will also check Marcus's ability to count forward and backward by walking a number line and identifying the matching equation. For instance, Marcus might be asked to start on 11 and add 3 more. He will first guess where he will land, and then actually walk to check his answer before finding a matching equation on the chalkboard. Marcus will earn a token for each correct response and will keep track of his tokens on the second monitoring chart (see Figure 3.5, p. 64). For more ideas on how to monitor and chart student progress, see Chapters 3 and 4 in *What Every School Leader Needs to Know About RTI* (Searle, 2010).

Once the learning target is set and clarified, a clear plan of action for reaching this goal is developed.

3.5 | Marcus's Self-Monitoring Chart for Number Line Use

Number of correct walks on number line						
5						
4					X	X
3			X			
2		X		X		
1	X					
Week #	1	2	3	4	5	6

Step 5. Select an Action Plan from a List of Options

Mrs. Ackerman and the problem-solving coach are ready to consider which interventions they should choose for Marcus's action plan. For the first four weeks, the teacher and coach decide to concentrate on strengthening Marcus's number sense, focusing ability, and self-monitoring skill. When they meet with Marcus and his parents, they discuss a variety of strategies for both home and school. Mrs. Ackerman selects classroom ideas from the list, the parents select what seems reasonable for them to do at home, and Marcus chooses things that he thinks will help him help himself. Figure 3.6 shows what they selected as starting strategies. After four weeks, they will look at the progress monitoring charts and decide how to expand or alter the plan.

Mrs. Ackerman and the problem-solving coach choose a CRA strategy to help Marcus develop his number sense. Because working with manipulatives can overload Marcus's delayed memory function, Mrs. Ackerman knows she must do plenty of modeling for Marcus to help him get comfortable with using them.

First, she models and then has Marcus use objects and numeral cards to label objects with a numeral as he counts orally. Marcus needs to realize that the last number said is the amount in the set (cardinality). She makes sure Marcus is constantly talking about what he is doing. She knows that students with memory deficits like Marcus need to articulate what they are doing to help them match language with the visual math. Mrs. Ackerman also finds that counting a variety of

3.6 | Action Plan for Marcus

Skills Needed	Teaching Strategies	Student Responsibilities	Suggestions for Parents
One-to-one correspondence to improve accurate counting (encoding)	• Model counting using concrete materials, pictures, and numerals as you have Marcus mimic each step you do. Slowly turn over more and more of the counting to him. • Model the games he is to play independently or with a partner at the math station.	• Match items to the number cards in the math station and check your work. • Play Chutes and Ladders with a friend. Make sure you count aloud as you move the correct number of spaces.	• Ask Marcus to do tasks like counting the silverware as he sets the table. Make sure he says a number as he puts down each piece.
Concept of greater and less than (working memory)	• Model doing greater-and-less-than problems by matching concrete materials and drawings. Show the matching equation. Ask Marcus to tell you how you can prove that set A is bigger than set B.	• Play a card game with a friend. Explain who wins each round by saying how many more or less the other person has.	• Ask questions like "Would you rather have the cup with 4 or 7 pieces of candy? Why?" Expect an answer like "I will take 4 because I don't like that kind of candy" or "I want 7 because that is 3 more than 4."
Counting up (working memory, visualization)	• Limit work to numerals between 0 and 20 for now. Model walking the number line to count x more or x less than the starting number. Help him match the math equation to his actions until he gets it.	• Practice walking the number line using self-check cards. • Play number line games with a friend. Count each number aloud as you add or subtract.	• Play any kind of game where counting is required, but don't always start at 1: "I am thinking of a number that is 3 more than 7. Tell me how you can figure out my number."
Ability to focus and keep track of where he is in a process and self-monitoring	• Either give him assignments with fewer problems (cut the paper in half and give the second half after the first is complete), or make a cardboard window that limits how much of the paper he can see at a time.	• Tell the teacher which strategy helps you keep track of where you are so you do not skip rows or problems. • Double-check to see if all your work is complete before handing it in.	• Play "What's missing?" games. Have Marcus look at a group of 5 or 6 items, then take one away and ask if he can identify what is missing.

real things in the environment and playing various counting games works better than using the same counting routine every day.

The next step in developing Marcus's number sense for greater and less than is to have him compare sets. Mrs. Ackerman starts with concrete objects (stars) and numeral labels (see Figure 3.7). She asks questions to guide his thinking: "How many are in each set? How do you know? Which set has more? Can you prove that to me? Which set has less? How do you know?" Repeated verbal practice games help firm up Marcus's vocabulary and his understanding of how the number system works.

When Marcus is solid on counting and comparing sets of concrete materials, Mrs. Ackerman will have him work with a partner to walk a number line and explain how they are counting up or down from a given number. Then she will talk him through the process: "Which number is bigger? How many more did you count up as you stepped from 9 to 11? That's right, so now you know that 11 is 2 more than 9. Predict where you will land if you walk 3 spaces to your right." Once this process makes sense to Marcus, she will ask him to write the math expressions that go with his walking. It is hard to be engaged in the lesson if the material doesn't make sense, but it is just as hard if the lesson seems boring or irrelevant, so Mrs. Ackerman will make up stories and games to go with the number line walking activities.

Large-Group Application

Even though Mrs. Ackerman was specifically targeting Marcus for improvement, she knows that there are other students whose number sense is still developing. After playing several number line games with the class, the "number line walk" became a station activity available for any student in the class.

At the number line station, students select math stories to solve from any of three baskets. The red basket is labeled "Getting Started," the green basket

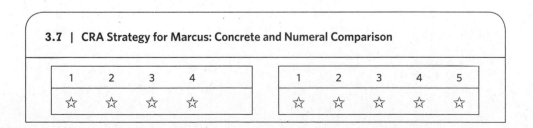

3.7 | CRA Strategy for Marcus: Concrete and Numeral Comparison

1	2	3	4
☆	☆	☆	☆

1	2	3	4	5
☆	☆	☆	☆	☆

is labeled "A Little Trickier," and the blue basket is labeled "Tough Problems." Any student may choose to work from any basket. After doing the activities and checking their own work, students can schedule a checkup with Mrs. Ackerman if they think they have had enough practice. Mrs. Ackerman pulls one of the stories from the basket and assesses whether the student has learned enough to earn the badge of honor for that level.

This differentiated station with tiered activities is helpful to all students and makes it easy for Mrs. Ackerman to provide extra support for students like Marcus.

Summary

Students who find math difficult may also be struggling with underactive memory systems. These students tend to give up easily, refuse to use math aids, rarely participate in class, procrastinate on assignments, refer to themselves as stupid, say they don't care, refuse to try homework, or simply do the minimum.

WHAT WORKS: Adjusting work that is too challenging by breaking it down into manageable pieces; modeling and practicing missing prerequisite skills using visuals and representations along with abstract symbols and numbers; encouraging verbalization of thinking and teaching students ways to ask for help; praising students' efforts; helping them see mistakes as opportunities to learn; not giving up on students even when they seem to want you to; applying a gradual release of responsibility.

WHAT DOESN'T WORK: Acting indifferent toward students when they appear unmotivated; going on when you know they don't understand basics; teaching only at the abstract level; not including guided practice and specific feedback in every lesson; making students feel that low grades are what they deserve; doing too much for students; being impatient or sarcastic.

We need to do whatever is necessary to see that students experience at least a 70–80 percent success rate daily, whether it is in academics or in handling social or emotional challenges. Success builds the motivation students need to keep trying to make positive changes. Repeated failure makes problems worse.

On Your Own

Now you are ready to practice applying the five-step method to our case study student, Beth, who is having some typical student issues.

Case study. *Beth is a student who always seems to be a million miles away during math class. She looks out the window, plays with her pencil, fails to complete assignments, never asks questions, and doesn't request help. She tries to make herself disappear by slouching down in her seat. When approached by the teacher, she becomes defensive and says, "This stuff is so boring."*

4

ORGANIZATION: HOW CAN I GET BETTER AT WRITING?

Julio would rather eat glass than write a story. Although generally described as a cooperative and friendly 3rd grader, when faced with written assignments, Julio shuts down. If pressed to write, he changes from an engaged learner to an uncooperative and even defiant child. He wants to write like other kids and has strong cognitive and linguistic skills, but his handwriting is awful, and he can't remember how to spell things. His teacher and parents have assured him that he can be a good writer if he will just try, but he still refuses.

Julio also has trouble keeping track of what he is supposed to be doing. Ninety percent of his classmates know the morning routine of putting their clothespin on the lunch count card, placing homework in the basket, taking their English books out, and editing the practice sentence on the board before class begins. For Julio, however, just getting to class with all of his homework and materials is an adventure. In his cubby and desk, old papers and notes create avalanches of clutter. The chaos contributes to other school problems, like not turning in his work and losing permission slips.

Loretta, who is in the 9th grade, has similar feelings about writing. Her parents and teachers often accuse her of being irresponsible and unmotivated because she seems to "forget" to do her work if anything but short answers are involved. Mr. West, her social studies teacher, notices that Loretta's note-taking skills are a disaster, so studying for a test seldom pays off in good grades. In Loretta's head, she isn't unmotivated. She sees herself as frustrated and overwhelmed by the mountain of writing assignments she receives. She cannot imagine how people think of enough things to write, so she just sits there or talks to her friends when she should be working. Loretta wishes her first drafts could be perfect, so she could just hand them in and be finished, but she knows she doesn't have the skills to pull that off.

She also accepts the adage that it is better to appear obnoxious than stupid, so she flat-out refuses to do writing assignments in class in front of her friends. She avoids looking stupid at all costs, even if that means cheating. This results in low grades for late and incomplete assignments as well as increasingly adversarial relationships with many of her teachers.

Neurological research shows that strategies that support the development of executive function are at the heart of student success in school (Cooper-Kahn & Dietzel, 2008). Executive skills like organization of time, ideas, tasks, and materials are too often not included in intervention plans, even when weaknesses in these areas prevent academics-focused interventions from working. It may seem like a waste of time to teach Julio how to keep his desk in order, but without working on this skill, he may never get the hang of organizing and managing anything, from thoughts in an essay to notes for a science test.

Root Causes of Poor Organization

Unless teachers help students see the connection between academic growth and use of organization strategies, success in both areas is often limited. In this chapter's opening case studies, both Julio and Loretta fail to hand in written assignments because they are avoiding work that requires difficult organizational tasks. In addition, delayed development of organization skills is affecting both students' self-confidence, which makes them harder to motivate than students who don't have these issues. Chances are you have had students in your class who are a lot like these two.

The first step in any solution is to identify specific reasons why the problems have been so difficult to solve. It's not that teachers haven't been trying to teach good organization and effective writing skills, so it must be deeper than what good basic instruction can accomplish. Talking about poor family support or a possible disability does not fall within our circle of influence, so our discussions will steer clear of those issues. Diagnosing possible reasons for poor organization and looking for specific gaps in writing skills is our plan of attack.

Use Figure 4.1 (p. 72) to help you identify the possible root causes of incomplete assignments due to poor organization. Which causes do you think fit our two students?

In Julio's case, the factors listed under "Cannot organize space and materials" will be the focus for his intervention plan. We'll see his teacher help him with sorting and classifying, identifying simple rules or patterns, and understanding why organizing space is important. For Loretta, teachers will concentrate on better organization of time (to help with meeting deadlines) and ideas (to help her break down complex tasks). Her problem-solving team will choose a few of the related causes listed under these focus issues to address one at a time. The column of factors under "Procrastinates" on the flowchart will be important for both students.

Let's look at a sampling of what research suggests are effective interventions for students who have trouble with organization, and select the ideas that are the best match for our case study students.

Interventions That Help with Organization

When the following research-based strategies are modeled and practiced, they help students unclutter their thinking and organize their time and work.

Getting Started: Prepare, Do, Check

I mentioned in Chapter 1 that although I am presenting the categories of executive function as distinct from one another, they often overlap, and the relationship between organization and planning is a prime example. A significant portion of organization has to do with planning and time management. I will offer one planning

4.1 | Root Causes of Poor Organization

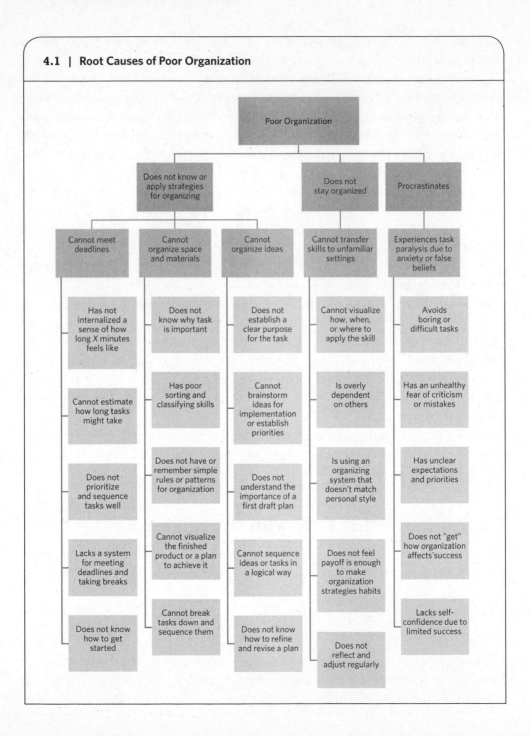

technique here (prepare, do, and check), but many more planning strategies are given in Chapter 2, and I recommend reviewing that fuller list of options when selecting interventions for your student.

Chances of work completion rise dramatically when students create a specific plan before they start working. Teaching three simple steps (prepare, do, and check) will help students like Loretta and Julio map out an entire process for getting assignments done. Checklists for each of the three steps follow. Remember to model and allow time for student practice.

For the *prepare* step,

1. Help students visualize the finished product and the steps for getting there to make the task of writing seem less overwhelming. Have students ask themselves, "What should this look like when it is completed, and what do I want people to say about my work? How long will this work take me?" According to Marzano and colleagues (2001), the more we use both linguistic and nonlinguistic representations, the better we are able to think and recall. Nonlinguistic representations like graphic organizers and rubrics stimulate and increase brain activity and help with visualization.

2. Use models and guided practice to help students break big tasks down into a written list of manageable parts (U.S. Department of Education, 2004).

3. Put "to do" lists on a timeline, including breaks. Gawande (2010) explains that human memory and attention can fail when you are performing either a high volume of simple tasks or a variety of complex tasks. Checklists and timelines help reduce errors.

4. Make sure students understand all directions. Tell them, "When in doubt, look about," or have them repeat directions to you or to a partner as a double-check for understanding (U.S. Department of Education, 2004).

5. Have students gather materials they will need and think of people and resources that can help if they get stuck (U.S. Department of Education, 2004).

For the *do* step,

1. Have students check things off the "to do" list as they complete them.
2. Remind students to avoid distractions—both things and people.
3. Help students plan small breaks but have a plan for getting right back to the job.

For the *check* step,

1. Have students make sure all "to do" steps from the checklist are finished.
2. Teach students to edit and revise for quality. Jim Wright (n.d.a) suggests that students develop an individualized checklist of the kinds of errors they commonly make on independent assignments and use a checklist of the four or five most common errors to help reduce or eliminate mistakes before turning in assignments.
3. Encourage students to make copies in case things get lost (for older students like Loretta).
4. Remind students to clean up the work space. (Make certain the schedule allows time for them to do this.)
5. Have students turn in the assignment. (It helps if there is a consistent place and time for this step.)
6. Suggest that students talk with an adult about what worked well and what didn't so they can make more efficient plans next time (Wright, n.d.a).

Sharing What to Do to Stay Organized

Getting organized is one thing; staying organized is quite another. When we are under pressure, we often revert to old patterns that feel right to us, so scheduling enough modeling, guidance, and practice to develop new organization habits that feel comfortable is critical to long-term change (Hattie et al., 1996).

To help your students develop good habits for organization, show them how you keep yourself organized, and then let class members brainstorm and share their own versions of the plan.

Here is one organizational strategy I demonstrated for my students. I create two sets of files: one set of 12 hanging files labeled with the months of the year, and one set of file folders labeled 1–31 for each day of the month. I file all material according to when it needs my attention. I place things I won't need until October in the "October" folder. When October arrives, I sort all the notes and papers into the files labeled 1–31 according to the exact day I plan to do something with them.

For example, if I need to submit a report by October 25th, I might drop my report form into the 18th file because that is the day I plan to start working on it. If I can't finish the report on the 18th, I refile it in the 19th file. When I pull that day's file, all my work is right there in front of me.

I explained to my students that this is the way many teachers and business-people make sure all parts of their job happen on time. The students then began talking about ways to use that type of thinking for their own organization. The results included everything from using my exact idea to using a paper or electronic calendar to break down and schedule both work and social events.

One key to helping students organize their thinking is scheduling enough time for them to design a plan. They need time to discuss pros and cons of specific strategies before deciding which one to try. They also need time at the end of every class to make sure they actually use their plan. Carving out time for this each day is difficult but essential for establishing good habits of organization. When students feel rushed, they default to old habits of "jam and go."

Finding and Matching the Student's Style

An organization system that works well *and* matches the student's style makes a big difference in whether or not the student sticks with it. It is good practice to model and suggest a variety of approaches to getting organized, but students need the opportunity to put together their own routines. It's all about ownership of the remedy. For instance, would it be better for Loretta to

- Use separate notebooks, use just one notebook with tabs, or use pocket folders?
- Put jobs on a timeline or make a checklist?
- Take notes using pictures, outlines, webs, color-coding, a word processor, or note cards?
- Study by rewriting notes or by making labels in margins?
- Study alone or with a partner?
- Make games or review notes with someone?
- Study in a quiet space or in a place that allows for interacting and asking questions?
- Take multiple short breaks or a few longer ones?

A great plan for you may not appeal to Loretta at all. One idea neurologist and teacher Judy Willis (2010b) recommends is to have students do a little active research to discover the study conditions that work best for them. Willis had students brainstorm a list of conditions for homework, and they came up with many possibilities: with or without music, with or without TV, with or without texting friends, in the kitchen, in bed, right after coming home from school, with snack breaks, studying for one long session, studying in smaller segments, studying alone or with a partner. Each day, students wrote down the starting and stopping times for their math homework and which conditions they chose for working. The next morning, students took a short quiz directly pulled from the homework. After recording and analyzing their results, each student drew conclusions from his or her personal data as well as the composite class data about the best conditions for doing homework. Designing a personalized system based on evidence of good results has a positive influence on motivation and increases students' sense of responsibility (Zimmerman & Schunk, 2001).

Creating Relevance by Charting Benefits

Julio needs to understand that taking control by organizing his materials, thoughts, and time minimizes "do-overs" and tendencies to drift off course that eat into his time to be creative and have fun. Having an awareness of the advantages of being organized will help him get past the "Who really cares and why do I need to do this?" stage.

For example, before Julio developed his organization plan, Miss Ritter timed how long it took him to find his supplies and get started on his math work on Monday and Tuesday. It took him about seven minutes to get started each day. On Tuesday afternoon, she helped Julio organize his materials and papers, and they created a "get ready quickly" checklist for him to use on Wednesday. Miss Ritter timed Julio again, and he saw that he was able to start in three minutes, which helped him finish in time to work at his favorite math work station. Miss Ritter has Julio chart these data daily so they can talk about how much time and effort he saves by using good organization skills. Seeing is believing, and this process pays off in both motivation and self-confidence. Studies (Fuchs & Fuchs, 1986) show as much as a 26-point gain in achievement when charting strategies are used properly.

Sorting and Classifying to Build Independence

Adults need to remember that even though it is far less hassle to organize the work and materials for students, especially elementary students, getting the work done is not the only objective. Learned helplessness is likely to set in when we do too much of the thinking, directing, and problem solving for students. Maintaining a careful balance between helping and guiding is key to promoting organized and independent thinking. Adults need to model, ask clarifying questions, and help students reflect on and adjust their own routines, not do the work for them.

For example, because Julio has a hard time finding things in his desk and cubby, Miss Ritter knows that the root cause of this problem is figuring out how to group items. She starts by having him sorting fun objects like marbles, chips, or crayons. She knows that it helps if you make the practice a game, like "guess the rule." She introduced the game to Julio like this:

> OK, Julio. Here's the deal. I am going to put these red, blue, green, and white chips in piles, and you have to guess what rule I'm using for organizing them. I'll start off easy, and then we will practice with harder things. You're correct; each pile has all the same color. Now, this next one will be a little trickier. Right again! Each pile has one chip of each color. Let's make it harder by putting chips and crayons together. Now what is the rule? Yes, all the red and green things are in one pile, and all the blue and white things are together in another. Now it's your turn. Put the piles together any way you want and see if I can guess the rule.

Once sorting and naming categories with a variety of fun items is comfortable for Julio, Miss Ritter explains that people use the same procedure to keep their supplies and materials organized so that they can find things easily. Next, she begins to play the rule game using "big things," "small things," and "very small things" as the categories, and they talk about how this kind of sorting helps with keeping desks and cubbies orderly: if big things stay on the bottom and small things are on the top, you are less likely to have your stuff fall out on the floor. If very small things are kept in a container, you can find them easily. Miss Ritter supervises the practice daily until she sees that Julio has it down and is ready to organize by size by himself or with a partner and needs only quality checks. Then it is time to graduate him to sorting papers in his folder.

Slow steps and continual practice with corrective feedback is what makes a skill become a habit. If time, practice, and reflection opportunities are not strong enough, Julio and his friends with the same issues will jump right back to squirreling things in whatever convenient spot they can find.

Breaking a Bad Habit: Procrastination

Just as important as teaching students to manage priorities is breaking habits that interfere with good organization. Blaming others and cramming too much into a schedule are habits that contribute to sloppy thinking, and procrastinating is another habit that interferes with good organization.

Procrastination often looks like lazy or unmotivated behavior, but many psychologists believe it is actually rooted in anxiety based on false beliefs (Szalavitz, 2003). Four anxiety issues are major contributors to procrastination:

- *Excessive fear* that there will be criticism for not being right the first time.
- *Avoidance* of difficult or boring tasks. (We all do this one at times.)
- *Unclear expectations,* which increase the odds for failure. (If everything is important, nothing is a priority.)
- *Depression,* which makes everything seem pointless; thus, very little feels fulfilling and many things seem out of control.

According to studies conducted by Carol Dweck (2006), a leading researcher in the field of psychology, these problems are often a result of people's beliefs about how smart they are and what personality traits they have. Some people believe that their basic intelligence and personal characteristics can't change. This is called a *fixed mind-set.* Other people believe that given enough personal effort, training, experience, and determination, they can expand their intellectual capacity and develop new ways of responding. This is called a *growth mind-set.*

It appears that Loretta, our student at the start of the chapter, has bought into the idea that her writing ability is fixed and therefore out of her control. She believes that if she is just not good at something, there is nothing she can do about it, so there is little future in trying hard. She wants to be "seen" as smart, or at least avoid looking dumb, so she gives up or cheats when faced with difficult work or chooses to only take on tasks that look like easy successes.

If Loretta can be convinced that being successful has more to do with her willingness to work hard and persist than with her innate ability to write, she will begin to hang in there even when faced with very tough problems. Dweck's research shows that students with growth mind-sets remain engaged when faced with challenging work. They also have no problem talking about their mistakes or admitting that they need help. This is what we want for Loretta.

Which interventions change a fixed theory of intelligence into a growth mind-set? Loretta's teachers and parents need to change both their language and their approaches to motivating her. First, they should stop trying to convince her that she is smart and start showing her that by continually working on the problem she can become much more skillful. They need to provide guided practice using a variety of problem-solving strategies. Loretta will also need to chart her own growth data so that she can confirm the fact that effort and guidance are increasing her level of success.

Adult supportive language needs to change from statements like "Look how fast you did that; you are so smart!" or "That was good work" to language that stresses effort—for example, "You really worked hard and organized carefully to get that answer. Which strategies did you use?" or "This is going to be challenging, but I know we can do this. Let's start together, and you can take over once you understand the little tricks I show you for making this work for you."

To foster strong growth mind-sets, adults need to avoid praising weak efforts or poor results. Feedback should specifically identify real strengths of the student's work as well as analyze exactly what kinds of things can be done to improve results. Emphasis should be placed on logical processes, personal effort, and good questions rather than on grades.

Root Causes of Poor Writing Skills

Loretta's and Julio's lack of organization skills affects their academic performance, but their troubles are not just due to late or incomplete assignments. Both have problems with any type of extended writing. Successful writing requires a great deal of planning and organization of thoughts, so it is not surprising that students with delayed executive function in these skills find writing unbearably difficult. If concentration is diverted to mechanics like forming letters and spelling, as it can be for beginning writers like Julio, sorting thoughts and ideas feels near impossible. Figure 4.2 (p. 80) is a flowchart to help with diagnosing root causes that may be holding up students with writing problems. Do you see any other categories that may be issues for Loretta and Julio?

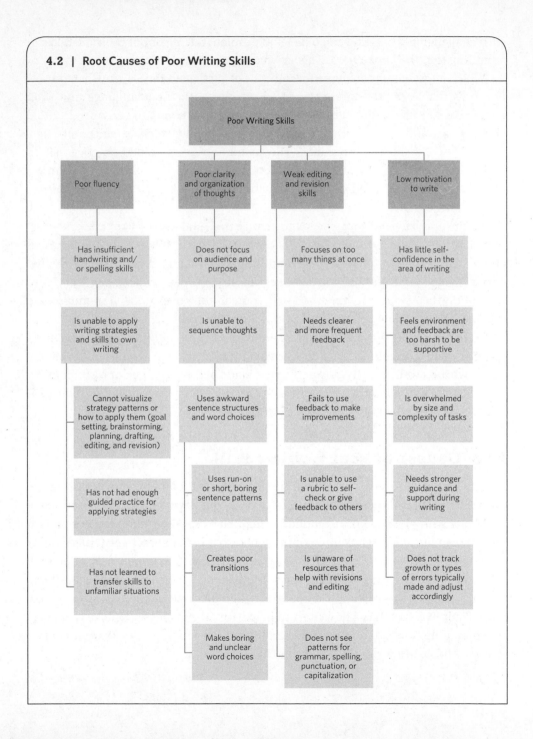

4.2 | Root Causes of Poor Writing Skills

Poor Writing Skills

Poor fluency

Has insufficient handwriting and/or spelling skills

Is unable to apply writing strategies and skills to own writing

Cannot visualize strategy patterns or how to apply them (goal setting, brainstorming, planning, drafting, editing, and revision)

Has not had enough guided practice for applying strategies

Has not learned to transfer skills to unfamiliar situations

Poor clarity and organization of thoughts

Does not focus on audience and purpose

Is unable to sequence thoughts

Uses awkward sentence structures and word choices

Uses run-on or short, boring sentence patterns

Creates poor transitions

Makes boring and unclear word choices

Weak editing and revision skills

Focuses on too many things at once

Needs clearer and more frequent feedback

Fails to use feedback to make improvements

Is unable to use a rubric to self-check or give feedback to others

Is unaware of resources that help with revisions and editing

Does not see patterns for grammar, spelling, punctuation, or capitalization

Low motivation to write

Has little self-confidence in the area of writing

Feels environment and feedback are too harsh to be supportive

Is overwhelmed by size and complexity of tasks

Needs stronger guidance and support during writing

Does not track growth or types of errors typically made and adjust accordingly

Interventions for Students with Poor Writing Skills

Have you ever stopped to think of all the skills, rules, and processes Julio and Loretta must combine and coordinate to write a simple paragraph? They must remember letter formation, spelling, grammar, capitalization, punctuation, sentence structure patterns, and vocabulary as they figure out ways to organize their ideas. And that's the *short* list. It's no wonder these students feel as though they are about to blow a cerebral fuse when we ask them to do complex writing assignments. Our interventions must make the fundamental processes of writing automatic enough that more mental energy is available to focus on the quality of the writing.

Tackling Handwriting

We know that handwriting is an issue for Julio, and we know that when students struggle with handwriting, they are more likely to have trouble switching their concentration back and forth between how to form letters, how to spell, and what they want to write (Graham & Weintraub, 1996). Research (Graham, Bollinger et al., 2012) suggests the following guidelines for improving handwriting:

- Julio will tire less easily if the movement for writing comes from his shoulder and forearm rather than from his fingers and wrist. Practicing in the air, writing big, and then gradually reducing the size of the gesture should help.
- The way that students grip a pencil varies widely according to personal preference (Berninger et al., 1996). If the grip Julio is using works, experts say leave him alone.
- Handwriting practice should start with single letters but progress quickly to copying and dictating words and sentences that students think are fun.
- Doing five to eight practices with one letter, then moving to another letter helps prevent fatigue and boredom.
- Engaging in multiple short writing sessions that use a consistent approach are better for developing motor memory than fewer long sessions. Kindergarten students should have 30 minutes of writing practice a day (in short sessions), and all others need an hour a day of combining handwriting and other types of writing skills across the curriculum.
- Direct instruction that initially focuses on penmanship, without the pressure of worrying about the writing content, is the most effective.

- Having students track their own growth by charting and analyzing their own data or portfolios has a positive effect on student progress and motivation.

Improving Spelling

Research (Graham, Harris, & Loynachan, 2012) shows that 850 words make up 80 percent of what elementary students write. Focusing on these words for spelling makes life easier on everyone. You can find this "basic spelling vocabulary list" at http://www.readingrockets.org. Here are some other recommendations I would try with Julio or any student who is having difficulty with spelling:

- Starting with invented spelling (spelling phonetically as best the writer can if stumped by a word) works for very beginning writers, early drafts, or personal pieces of writing because it minimizes interruptions to the flow of ideas. Corrections always need to be made during the editing stage if the final product is to be published or shared to avoid the "it's close enough for me" attitude from developing.
- Research (Hughes & Searle, 1997) shows that the exploratory approach to spelling works best for most students. This method encourages students to identify patterns in words (phonetic, word families, syllables, and affixes). Severely struggling spellers like Julio will need repeated modeling and guided practice for pattern recognition.
- Instruction should quickly shift the focus from spelling words in isolation to applying correct spelling in the student's own writing (Graham, Bollinger et al., 2012).
- Access to word walls (collections of organized words prominently displayed for students to refer to while writing) helps students with tough words. Just make sure this is not the only strategy used.
- Students like Julio should keep a log of frequently misspelled words and error patterns to help them set goals and track their personal progress on these words (U.S. Department of Education, 2004). Miss Ritter will help Julio create a personal spelling dictionary that puts his list of spelling demons in alphabetical order so that he can study and refer to them as needed when he is writing.

Using a spell checker in a word-processing program is useful, but teachers should explain the limitations of this tool. If the student doesn't have a clue how to spell the word or cannot recognize the correct word when the spell checker offers options, this tool is of little help. In addition, the spell checker misses misspellings when the word is a real word but not used correctly: sew, spell check will knot sea the miss takes that eye halve maid inn this sentence.

Introducing the Sloppy Outline

Sloppy outlines are a great tool to help students like Loretta consider all the factors in planning for writing. These outlines support students in deciding what to write, what strategies to use, and how the purpose and audience affect writing style and word choice—all considerations that help students organize the writing process. They are called "sloppy" because they are for working ideas out, a messy process that involves changes; they are not final products. Sharing this strategy with a chart of the outline categories and a verbalization of how you might make choices in each category provides the best introduction. But to be truly effective, this strategy must be followed up with opportunities for students to immediately apply what is modeled.

Figure 4.3 (p. 84) shows Mr. West's steps of a sloppy outline with the accompanying think-aloud he used to model this process for Loretta. Using think-alouds to make thoughts transparent for the student is helpful in every content area, but the technique is particularly illuminating for writing (Gibson, 2012). The steps in the figure are designed to help a writer plan a fiction piece but can be adapted for nonfiction by changing the category of "character development" to "key points" to be elaborated on in an essay.

Loretta finds this approach to writing exciting because it breaks the writing process down into simple-to-follow steps, and she doesn't have to bother writing a complete sentence until she has revised, organized, and elaborated on her ideas several times.

Giving Students Choices

After modeling or brainstorming ideas and strategies (like the sloppy outline) for organizing their writing, give students a choice of topics or approaches to use in their assignments. Offering choices increases the likelihood that the student will see the assignment as relevant (Glasser, 1998). Make certain the criteria for quality are clear and fit the student choices.

4.3 | Sample Sloppy Outline

Six Writing Steps	Teacher's Think-Aloud
1. Purpose	I want this story's purpose to be "to entertain my audience," so I need to make this fun to read.
2. Audience	I will write it so it appeals to middle school kids. That means it has to be about something they can relate to. Maybe I'll use a sibling who is a pain as my main idea.
3. Character development	OK, now I need to describe this sibling. I'll use brainstorming and make a list that will create a good picture. First, I think I'll choose a girl who is about 6 years old. She gets good grades. She likes dolls. She'll have red hair, blue eyes, short fingers, and a little nose. She rides a bike and likes to skate. She will be thin and wear blue jeans and sneakers. I'll make her short, and I think I'll give her freckles. That's a good start.
4. Delete ideas that don't fit	I think there are a few ideas in my list I don't need just to introduce my character. I will scratch off the grades. I'm not sure her short fingers add anything, so I'll scratch that off the list, too.
5. Clarify and pair ideas	Let's see, how can I make this list more interesting to my reader? I'll write adjectives I like next to the words on my list. I think I'll make her have "devilish" blue eyes. She can have "long, red" pigtails and a "pug" nose. Her blue jeans will have a "hole in the knee," I'll call her "skinny" instead of thin. Let's make those sneakers "light-up sneakers with magic-marker stars."
6. Sequence the ideas and read the description	OK, by just looking at my sloppy outline, I can try reading what I think it will sound like. My description will read something like this: "My little sister is the picture of trouble. She is a skinny little 6-year-old with long, red—wait, I think I'll change that to "flaming"—with flaming red pigtails and a little pug nose covered with freckles. Her devilish blue eyes let you know that she is usually up to something. The holes in her blue jeans are a result of the many spills she has taken as she rides her bike." Maybe "tears around on her bike" sounds better. I like that. I'm ready to write this paragraph down. See, I have a good start and have revised my thoughts several times without putting one sentence on paper yet. Works for me!

For instance, expanding on the sample sloppy outline, I might say, "Now I want you and your partner to use the same six-step process I just modeled to create your own purpose, audience, and character. You may choose to develop a character for your own story, or you may create another character for me to use in mine."

Practicing Sentence Structure

Sentence structure practice has a positive influence on both the quality and the quantity of writing a student does. This type of practice includes three main strategies (Wright, n.d.b), including

1. Sentence combining, or saying the same thing in fewer words.
2. Identifying run-on sentences to break down into shorter, clearer sentences.
3. Sentence editing to replace or add words and check for the correct use of writing conventions (spelling, grammar, capitalization, and punctuation).

Miss Ritter explains to Julio's writing group that sentence combining makes monotonous writing more interesting for the reader by adding variety. The think-aloud she uses to demonstrate this skill sounds like this:

> Let's look at the story I wrote this morning: "I have a dog. He is a cocker spaniel. He likes to chase a ball. He hates cats." Do you like it? What suggestions do you have for making it more interesting? Yes, I agree. My sentences are too short and choppy. Let me show you how I would think of a better way to say the same thing. Let's see. If I look at the first two sentences, I think they would sound better if I put them together. I could just say, "I have a cocker spaniel." Let me see if I can add my third sentence to this. What if I say, "I have a cocker spaniel who likes to chase a ball"? That sounds even better. I believe I can even add the fourth sentence to this and make it say, "I have a cocker spaniel who likes to chase a ball, but if he sees a cat, he will take off like a shot." Do you see what I did to get a more interesting sentence? You can go too far with that and make your sentence what we call a *run-on,* but we will talk about that tomorrow. Let's just practice combining sentences with a partner today. You will do the same thing I just did, and I want to hear your thinking.

You can find some helpful sentence-combining exercises on the web at http:// grammar.about.com/od/tests/a/introsc.htm.

Making the Criteria for Quality Clear

Before students can be expected to edit their own work, they need a clear idea of what great work looks like. Just telling them is not enough; they need to see it and internalize what constitutes quality. Rubrics are one of the most effective tools for sharing criteria for written work with students. Two websites that I have found helpful for designing rubrics are Kathy Schrock's Guide to Everything (http://www. teachnology.com/web_tools/rubrics/handwriting/) and Rubistar (http://rubistar. 4teachers.org/index.php).

Once Mr. West has developed a rubric that describes exactly what constitutes a good writing assignment, he is ready to use anonymous papers from previous classes to give his students practice in interpreting and applying this rubric. He starts with an excellent paper and has students work with partners to agree on the type of feedback they think this student needs. Mr. West then shares his own feedback recommendations to help students clarify and adjust the way they are interpreting the rubric. The next paper students are asked to analyze is one that needs more corrections than the first. The third paper needs even more adjustments. By the time students have gone through this process three times, they generally understand how to identify both strengths and opportunities for improvement for all levels of papers. Now Loretta and her classmates are ready to do peer reviews.

Revising and Editing Practice

Students can typically identify problems in other people's writing more easily than they can in their own, but with guidance, they can start applying what they've learned during peer feedback sessions to their own work. When implemented correctly, peer revision sessions reinforce powerful writing strategies and create a community of writers who help and support one another. Because this process provides an authentic audience, it generally has a positive effect on motivation, especially for grades 4 and up, when rules and procedures emphasize kind and constructive comments (Graham, Bollinger et al., 2012). Here is a basic peer revision and editing procedure that I use:

1. The author reads his or her work to the peer editors. (I generally assign two editors to each author.)

2. Student editors share only what they like best about their partner's writing and why.
3. Editors silently reread the work and make a list of questions to ask the author that will help him or her revise the content and structure of the work, such as "What were you trying to make the reader feel in this paragraph?" or "What words could help your readers see what you are describing more clearly?"
4. The author makes appropriate revisions to the content.
5. The author meets again with student editors to jointly work on finding and correcting errors in mechanics, such as sentence structure, grammar, punctuation, capitalization, and spelling.

Creating a Safe Learning Environment

Students need multiple safe interactions with teachers and other students as they write. Initial practices should not be graded. If the feedback is timely (given as they work or by the next period); specific (including precise suggestions, not grades); and manageable (not including more information than students can process), students are more likely to understand that mistakes and corrections are an important part of the process for all writers (Dean, Hubbell, Pitler, & Stone, 2012).

Lending Relevance with a "Real" Audience

Publishing for a viable audience makes writing authentic and engaging. Talk to students about how much people have to write to communicate in daily life (e.g., e-mail messages, blog posts, letters, grocery lists, "how to" directions, stories) and why that writing needs to be clear. Invite people from the community to read the students' work and comment on it. My students were not particularly motivated when they heard that they had to build a paper airplane and give a report defending their design until I mentioned that two employees from Wright Patterson Air Force Base had agreed to give them feedback. All of a sudden, the task took on a new level of importance.

Using websites designed to help students collaborate or share their ideas with an audience also creates relevance. Students can post their writing and invite other students to comment and make suggestions at http://voicethread.com. To practice "how to" writing, they can record (both visually and auditorily) a lesson to share at http://www.showme.com.

Five-Step Problem-Solving Case Study: Poor Organization and Writing Skills

Now let's see how all this information on improving organization and writing skills can be applied to our case study student, Liz.

Liz is struggling, especially in Miss DiSalle's 7th grade English class. Even though she is quick to answer questions during class, Liz chooses to do the minimum when it comes to any kind of written work. All of her teachers notice that her writing, vocabulary, and sentence structure are weak, and her answers are seldom a good match to the questions asked. She chooses to write in short, choppy bullet points, and it seems like any random thing she can remember goes into her answer. She is also chronically late with assignments. When she does hand in assignments, more than half of them are incomplete.

Step 1. Know the Student

Miss DiSalle meets with Mr. Bowers, the head of the English department, who has been trained to be a problem-solving coach. They start their discussion by identifying concerns about Liz's behavior and academic performance and listing her strengths. They record all this information in a chart (see Figure 4.4).

4.4 | Strengths and Concerns Chart for Liz

Name: Liz Lange
Grade: 7

Academic concerns:	Behavior concerns:
• Poor composition skills • Poor editing and revising effort • Weak vocabulary • Weak note-taking skills	• Poor attitude about doing written assignments • Gives up easily on written work • Sassy with teachers when corrected • Lots of incomplete and missing assignments
Strengths to build on:	
• Is willing to participate in class discussions • Can spell, capitalize, and punctuate well • Reads on grade level	• Has many friends • Loves animals; wants to be a vet • Has beautiful penmanship

Step 2. Analyze the Root Causes

The flowchart showing root causes of organization problems (Figure 4.1) and the flowchart for root causes of writing problems (Figure 4.2) will guide the discussion about what to focus on to improve Liz's persistent writing, attitude, and organization problems. The first conversation between Miss DiSalle and the coach to diagnose issues goes like this:

Coach: Why do you think Liz has so many missing writing assignments?

Miss DiSalle: I think she is just lazy and has a stubborn streak. If teachers tell her to get busy, she just shuts down and often refuses to even pick up a pen.

Coach: In her mind, what does Liz achieve by "shutting down"?

Miss DiSalle: I don't know. Maybe she is protecting a fragile ego since she writes so poorly. It's not like she doesn't know the material. She does extremely well in class discussions. That is what makes her attitude so hard to tolerate.

Coach: So she knows the content but cannot put her thoughts on paper?

Miss DiSalle: I don't know if it is "cannot" or "will not." I know she hates to write and complains that she can never think of anything to say, so she writes a few phrases and gives up.

Coach: OK, let's approach this as a "cannot" issue instead of an attitude problem for now. What could be blocking Liz from wanting to try?

Miss DiSalle: Maybe she doesn't know how to focus her writing. Her sentences sound like a 3rd grader wrote them, and her answers often don't address the point, so on the writing chart [Figure 4.2], it looks like "Does not focus on audience and purpose" is probably the best fit.

Coach: So if we fix the sense of audience and purpose, do you think that will improve her poor record of completing assignments?

Miss DiSalle: I think that will help focus her writing, but there is still the problem of her refusing to do the work and just forgetting her assignments regularly.

Coach: Why do you think that happens?

Miss DiSalle: I think part of it is that she doesn't know how to organize her thoughts, and the other part is not having a system for pacing her time or prioritizing her work.

Coach: So working on her organization of both time and ideas as we strengthen her writing strategies sounds like the plan?

Miss DiSalle: Yes, I think generating and organizing ideas around the purpose of the assignment has to be the first step. We can also work on helping her develop a system for recording assignments and double-checking for completeness.

Coach: It's going to take support from all the teachers to give her enough practice in both writing and organization to make a difference. We may also need a tutor to work with her for a few minutes during study hall for reinforcement and feedback. Is there a student or aide we could train to do that? Training for every teacher on ways to help her define her purpose for writing and manage her assignments will be essential for consistency.

When Miss DiSalle first saw the writing flowchart, she thought that the handwriting/spelling box was the only issue that did not apply to Liz, but she was smart enough to realize that working on too many things at once can make things worse. Miss DiSalle decided to set priorities and pick off the troublesome areas a few at a time.

Step 3. Set a Clear and Measurable Goal

Because meeting deadlines—especially for written assignments—is causing problems in all content areas, Miss DiSalle helps Liz select one assignment management procedure to start with. Liz also has no idea where to begin when it comes to written assignments, so Miss DiSalle chooses a goal for learning to brainstorm ideas to go with the goal for clarifying audience and purpose. Next, Miss DiSalle and the coach formulate a hypothesis about how addressing these issues will affect Liz's work and determine what the goal for improvement will be.

> **Hypothesis:** If we teach Liz ways to brainstorm ideas, clarify her purpose for writing, and manage her assignments more effectively, she should be able to increase the number of successfully completed writing assignments.
>
> **Time frame and measurement benchmarks:** Within six weeks, we should see an increase in complete assignments handed in on time going from 45 percent to 75 percent, and Liz will be able to describe how her written response is appropriate for both the purpose and the audience.

A 75 percent target would be too steep for many students to hit in just six weeks, but since Liz knows the material, Miss DiSalle did not think this would look like an unreachable goal to Liz. Setting the goal too high or too low can adversely affect not only achievement but also motivation to even try.

4.5 | Liz's Self-Monitoring Chart for Completion and Focus of Written Assignments

		Monday	Tuesday	Wednesday	Thursday	Friday
Social Studies	Completed assignments	Yes No	Yes No	Yes No	Yes No	Yes No
	Written response matches the purpose and audience	Yes No	Yes No	Yes No	Yes No	Yes No
Science	Completed assignments	Yes No	Yes No	Yes No	Yes No	Yes No
	Written response matches the purpose and audience	Yes No	Yes No	Yes No	Yes No	Yes No
Art	Completed assignments	Yes No	Yes No	Yes No	Yes No	Yes No
Language Arts	Completed assignments	Yes No	Yes No	Yes No	Yes No	Yes No
Math	Completed assignments	Yes No	Yes No	Yes No	Yes No	Yes No

Once the goals are set, a measuring tool that allows Liz and her teachers to visualize the progress or lack of it is critical to implementation. If after six weeks they see no measurable growth, they have probably selected the wrong strategies or even the wrong goal. The rule is "Don't continue to do what is not working." This sounds like common sense, but unfortunately it is not always common practice.

Step 4. Decide How to Monitor Student Progress

Helping Liz chart her own growth will add strength to the intervention plan. Figure 4.5 is an example of the chart Miss DiSalle designed with Liz's input. Liz's writing improvement will be measured by how clearly she matches her writing to the purpose and audience. She will track this progress in social studies and science classes for six weeks, even though all teachers are helping with the intervention. Her improvement in managing her written work will be reflected in her ability to complete and hand in her written assignments in all listed content areas.

When Liz's writing becomes clearer on addressing the purpose and audience, the teachers will switch the focus to other key skills, like elaboration of ideas or improving sentence structure. The next step is to check the database of researched ideas to find strategies that fit Liz's case.

Step 5. Select an Action Plan from a List of Options

Making significant progress in writing requires a big time commitment—at least an hour a day, using many different contexts, for six to nine weeks. This means teachers in all content areas need to cooperate with implementing parts of the plan to ensure that the student gets enough instruction and practice. Figure 4.6 (p. 92) shows Liz's beginning action plan.

One reason Liz sees writing as a task to tolerate and get through is that she doesn't think her writing matters. Teaching students how to use their writing to impact others can go a long way toward helping them get excited about doing it.

4.6 | First Writing and Organization Action Plan for Liz

Skills Needed	Teaching Strategies	Student Responsibilities	Suggestions for Parents
Figuring out what to write	• Model and practice ways to get ideas for writing different types of texts: 1. Brainstorming 2. Researching 3. Discussion with others 4. Reading other people's writing to get ideas • Discuss the fact that all people find focusing on what to write difficult and need to develop strategies to help themselves.	• Start by keeping a list of writing ideas in your journal for each class. • List each of the four strategies for getting ideas that you practiced with your teacher and identify situations where you might use them, either in class or at home.	• Show Liz how you generate your ideas when you need to write (e.g., shopping lists, letters, reports).
Organizing ideas into drafts	• Model how to use graphic organizers like timelines to sequence ideas or use webs to show relationships. Have Liz use graphic organizers to create visuals of how her ideas flow and match the purpose. Turn some of the plans into actual written texts. • Use a "sloppy outline" to model how to create a draft for a paper that is due in your class.	• Select a graphic organizer and redo the notes from one of your classes. This will help you review the content and see how ideas fit together. Use this information to generate questions you need to ask before the test or before writing your report.	• Show Liz how you organize your ideas before you take action (e.g., a diagram before moving furniture or a list of activities before a party).

(continued)

4.6 | First Writing and Organization Action Plan for Liz   *(Continued)*

Skills Needed	Teaching Strategies	Student Responsibilities	Suggestions for Parents
Writing for a purpose and an audience	• Model ways to figure out the author's purpose. Have Liz identify the purpose and audience of several types of texts or media. Give immediate feedback. • Use a think-aloud strategy to model how changing a piece's audience and purpose often requires a change of tone or word selection. For example, write the same information for both an adult and a preschooler. • Have Liz revise a piece of writing to suit a kindergarten class. Ask a kindergartner to read the revision to Liz. Ask questions to see if the revision really helped the child understand. This will emphasize how different the writing is when the audience changes. Write the same piece and adjust to suit an older student.	• Make a three-column chart. In column one, list different goals for writing (persuade, inform, reflect, entertain). In the second column, list audiences you might write for (blog visitors, newspaper readers, parent, teacher, classmates, politicians, self). In the third column, note things to keep in mind when writing for each type of audience and purpose. • Identify your purpose and audience before you begin to write. Keep checking back to make sure you are keeping them in mind.	• Read Liz's report and summarize the main points for her. Tell her how the writing made you feel about the topic so she can see if her audience is likely to respond the way she intended. Avoid editing comments at this point and focus on the content. (A video example of the teacher doing this with Liz will be sent home.)
Organizing assignments	• Have classmates demonstrate several techniques they use for recording and double-checking assignments. Have them discuss the pros and cons of each system and then design a procedure they think will work for them. Check in with Liz to make sure she follows through with her new system each day until it becomes a habit.	• After listening to various organization ideas, develop your own system. Show your parents and teachers how it is working, or ask for help adjusting it as needed. • Keep your growth chart to show how the system is helping you get your completed assignments in on time.	• Show Liz how you organize your tasks using calendars, charts, and lists. • Ask Liz to explain her assignment organization system. Each Wednesday, review how it is working and help her make adjustments as needed.

Miss DiSalle starts out by helping Liz identify the purposes of other writers' work. As Liz looks at magazine ads and YouTube clips, Miss DiSalle asks questions like, "Who do you think is the target audience here? What point is this author making? What do you think the writer wants this audience to think, feel, or decide to do? How is the author making this emotion happen for the audience?" Some of the writing samples Miss DiSalle uses are persuasive, some are informative, others are descriptive, and a couple tell a story. This exercise helps Liz see how writers can approach the same topic in different ways depending on their audience and on what impact they want to have on their audience.

Liz found this task to be highly engaging and has agreed to lead it for a group of students in her class. After analyzing other writers' target audiences and purposes, the group members will create their own concise and powerful ads or scripts for producing video clips. Their purpose and audience can be anything from trying to convince the cafeteria supervisor to put tablecloths and flowers on tables to posting a description of life in a U.S. middle school on an international blog. These tasks hardly seem like writing assignments to Liz, yet she is learning the most essential element of writing: focus on a purpose and make sure it has the intended effect on your reader.

Large-Group Application

Liz's teachers each chose specific strategies for writing that focused on purpose and audience and suited their respective content areas. They will present some of this instruction to the whole class and reinforce some of it in small groups, or possibly just with Liz.

Liz's math teacher chose to focus on teaching students to take notes with a clear purpose in mind. He knows that the Common Core standards require students to write clear explanations of their processes and thinking, so this is something he planned to include in his instruction anyway. On some days, he focuses Liz on taking notes to help an absent student catch up, and on other days she takes notes to compare what she saw as critical information against the notes of another student who is good at math. Liz sees that the detail required for each type of note taking is different depending on her intended purpose and audience.

The science teacher decides to concentrate on the prewriting strategy of making lists of key ideas, sequencing them, and adding descriptive words. He challenges his students to use this outline to write lab reports so clearly that another student team can repeat the investigation just from using the first team's notes. This models the work of real scientists, so the students see the purpose of accuracy and detail in their writing. This strategy worked so well that the teacher decided to make it a regular part of his weekly review process for all students.

The social studies teacher agreed to model brainstorming and some simple research strategies (using only two sources) to help Liz and a few other students plan their approaches to the two reports coming up in the next four weeks. Liz will work with a partner as she gathers and records her information. Her purpose for gathering the information is to write a one-minute ad trying to convince people to support or take a stand against the actions of a political figure the class is studying. Her audience changes from one week to the next. Sometimes she has to convince the principal, and at other times students in the 6th grade. Students use peer reviews to make revisions and test the power of their statements, but students must write the ads on their own before performing or recording them.

The study hall teacher is going to touch base with Liz to make sure she remembers and is applying the research and writing steps properly. This will help Liz articulate how she plans to organize and word her report, keeping in mind the purpose and audience of the assignment. The teachers who ask the guiding questions do not do the actual work with Liz; they just help her keep her focus.

The art teacher plans to work on helping Liz with her organization skills by having her make clear checklists for the materials she needs for class each day. The teacher is also helping the entire class use a daily reflection notebook to list procedures and organize ideas they find helpful in art class. At the end of each month, the students will write a description of the procedure they find to be most helpful. They will give their compilation of the "best tips" to the incoming class of art students.

Miss DiSalle is planning to model and practice each of the selected strategies with Liz and three other students in her English class. During the first four weeks of intervention, the focus will be on ways to generate, organize, and clarify ideas for writing, with an emphasis on writing with a clear sense of purpose and audience. Then the focus will switch to using a variety of sentence structures to increase the impact of writing. More than half the class will be included in these lessons. Miss DiSalle will also work on modeling and monitoring Liz's assignment organization chart and checklist for completed work.

Summary

When poor organization and weak composition skills are combined, the outcome is usually poor grades across the board and students with defeatist attitudes. Careful reteaching of strategies, such as brainstorming, use of graphic organizers, draft creation, sentence building, and editing and revising are key components for writing interventions. With so much academic ground to cover, teachers might be tempted to go too fast for students with limited capacity to keep ideas and materials organized. There is much truth in the saying that "trying to do everything results in accomplishing little." The best approach is to identify and concentrate on a few important things until students have mastered the skill and are able to apply it without needing to think it through each time. Only then does adding a new skill make sense.

WHAT WORKS: Teaching sorting and categorizing skills; modeling rather than explaining expectations; building in student choices for types of writing assignments and topics; having authentic audiences for writing; conducting small-group discussions about ways to generate ideas and organize thoughts; providing frequent corrective feedback during the writing process; demonstrating how to organize thoughts using a sloppy outline before writing any sentences.

WHAT DOESN'T WORK: Labeling students as irresponsible without checking to see if the skills are in place; having unclear expectations; grading all papers without allowing for practice assignments; lecturing until the end of class so students have no time to sort and organize; giving long-term assignments without checking to see if students can develop a plan for completing them; assigning topics students have no interest in; allowing repeated failures to happen without reteaching and giving opportunities for recovery; not coordinating with teachers in other subject areas.

Helping students with organization is difficult if one of the related problems is the inability to focus attention. In Chapter 5, we will look at root causes of focusing problems in general and concentrate on how these issues affect students with reading difficulties.

On Your Own

Below are three case studies that might remind you of an actual student in your school. Select one case and practice using the five-step problem-solving process. If you want to use data based on your own student, you may find the process even easier to manage.

Case study 1. *James has a low tolerance for working on writing assignments. He can tell you what he intends to say if you have a prewriting conversation with him, but he tends to forget his plan as soon as he starts putting things on paper. His stories end up being one big awkward sentence with little to no punctuation or capitalization. He writes as few words as possible, and his handwriting is difficult to decipher.*

Case study 2. *Mary is a cooperative student who starts out giving her best effort but soon loses her enthusiasm as she struggles to put her thoughts into writing. Mary tries to play it safe by sticking to words she can spell, so her writing tends to be short and boring. When the teacher hands back the draft, Mary feels like crying because her paper is always covered with red correction notes. Mary pulls herself together and tries to use these notes to make her revisions, but sadly, her second attempts are barely better than her original drafts.*

Case study 3. *Brandon has both attitude and organizational issues, especially when it comes to doing written tasks. He misses a lot of school and believes that a good offense is his best defense against having to do his work. When asked for his assignments, he either claims that he didn't know anything was due because he wasn't in school or says that he isn't a good writer so everybody can just "forget it." Brandon is an extremely bright student, but he hasn't a clue about how to approach complex writing assignments, so he doesn't.*

FOCUSING ATTENTION: WHAT DID YOU SAY AND WHY CAN'T I READ?

Catherine isn't fitting in very well in her new high school. She doesn't see that her shyness often comes off as snobbery. She watches other kids have fun but can't imagine what she needs to do to fit in. She hasn't figured out that failing to show up or breaking promises upsets people. Catherine also doesn't pick up on the negative responses people have when she sulks or doesn't get her way. Often after dinner, Catherine is totally unaware that her mother is giving her "the look" because she is sitting at the table as the rest of the family helps with the dishes. This same lack of attention to detail causes Catherine problems with schoolwork. She glosses over information and tough vocabulary when she reads, which interferes with her comprehension. She doesn't pick up on the details during instruction, which means her notes are spotty and her work is marginal. Her homework is frequently missing or incomplete because she doesn't catch the assignment details, either.

Cheree is very comfortable with the classroom routine set up in Mrs. Barton's 2nd grade, but today there is a substitute teacher who is doing things all wrong. Cheree keeps telling him, "That is not the way Mrs. Barton wants us to do this," but the sub won't listen to her. Cheree is on the verge of a full-blown meltdown. This same rigid thinking happens in math class when the teacher asks her to solve a problem another way, or in reading when the teacher wants her to think of a different ending for a story. Cheree is also struggling with reading fluency. She recognizes lots of words on flashcards, but her reading is so choppy that the story usually doesn't make sense to her.

Lance has always had a hard time concentrating, but 5th grade work is proving to be even more of a challenge. When he thinks the presentations and reading assignments are uninteresting or too challenging, Lance either slinks quietly into the happy place in his head or creates his own fun by disrupting the class. Fooling around reduces his frustration and boredom but results in poor grades. His lack of focus on rules and procedures leads him to blurt out answers or talk excessively, making him a "frequent flyer" to the office.

Why do the teachers have to talk so much and give so many boring assignments? Lance used to like school, but now he hates it. There is just too much reading, and he isn't any good at that. When he tries to read, it seems as though his mind keeps drifting in and out. He sounds like a fluent reader, but when he comes to the bottom of the page, he doesn't have a clue about what he just read. Every day, Lance has intentions of listening more closely and doing better work, but his priorities seem to turn on a dime, and then there he is, in the office again.

These three students don't sound much alike: Catherine is oblivious, Cheree is rigid, and Lance is disruptive. But all three have delays in the same aspect of executive function: the ability to focus attention. They also have an academic problem in common. Knowing what to focus on, how to sift information, and how to shift attention are skills necessary for reading comprehension. Like many students with focus issues, Catherine, Cheree, and Lance are struggling to understand what they read.

Root Causes of Poor Attention and Focus

Unproductive activity is typical for students with executive attention and focusing problems. They cannot stay centered on important issues, and they overlook critical details. They drift off course, especially when they don't see the importance of the activity. These students' brains don't tolerate uninteresting material or exercises as well as others' do. Their lack of work completion is not simply procrastination. Their inability to focus, sustain concentration, and transition from one activity to another causes an enormous amount of frustration every day. Students who experience the stress of poor focusing and transitioning skills often feel the need to shut the world out or let their inner Vesuvius blow. Neither of these choices really solves the problem, but they are the only options these students see.

Analyzing the underlying issues at work when students are inattentive can help teachers offer alternatives. Figure 5.1 is a root causes chart to help you identify some of the specific executive function issues that cause weak attention control. Remember to look for skill gaps that seem to match our case study students.

By their very nature, students tend to have wandering minds and spontaneous thoughts, but for students like Lance who have executive dysfunction, the spontaneity and shortened windows of concentration are especially problematic. A small distraction, like a dime on the floor, leads to a three-minute mental debate about whether to pick up the dime now or later. Meanwhile, the teacher has finished explaining the directions for the reading assignment. Getting Lance's attention is one thing, but keeping him focused is even harder. He wants to be a good student, but he runs out of mental energy when the tasks are long or complex. He also needs much more mental stimulation to maintain his focus than most other students do.

Cheree's inability to switch her focus is responsible for her difficulties and makes her appear rigid, inflexible, and slow to change. Cheree can't adjust familiar routines and rules to fit changing circumstances. When the kids on the playground want to change the rules for playing a game, Cheree digs in her heels and objects. She reacts by screaming, "Nobody ever listens to me! You all hate me!" Obviously, this kind of outburst creates new problems. Students begin seeing Cheree as a nutcase and want to exclude her, thus reinforcing her extreme and unbending viewpoint of how they feel about her. This "my way or the highway" thinking not only causes social problems but is also a barrier to complex problem solving.

In academic work, Cheree's lack of mental flexibility makes it hard for her to see things from different points of view. When asked to analyze how a character feels or why something happens in a science investigation, she thinks of one idea and stops there. Since your first idea seldom is your best idea, this kind of thinking doesn't work out very well. Flexible thinkers are able to consider several solutions

5.1 | Root Causes of Poor Attention and Focus

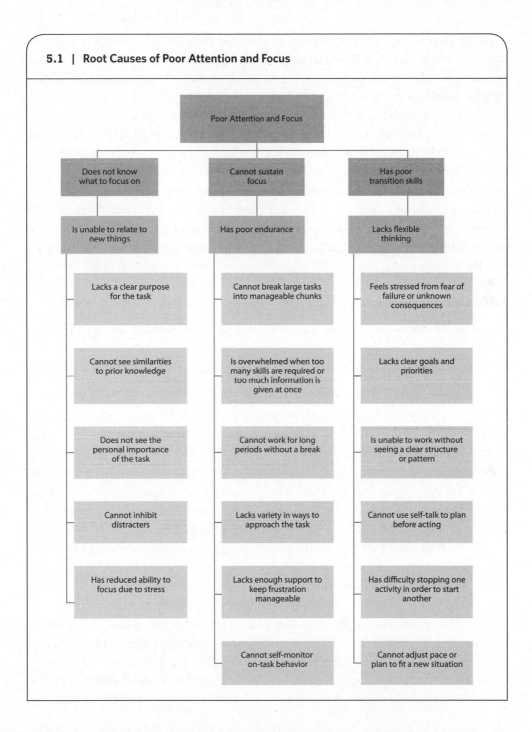

or possible consequences before acting. Because of Cheree's inability to shift her thinking beyond her initial impulse, she ends up making many bad choices. This problem also keeps her from applying skills she knows in isolation to unfamiliar or more complex work.

Catherine's inability to establish focus on important information and salient details makes her friends, family, and teachers think she is apathetic and insensitive. In reality, she has trouble picking up on the purpose of their communication, relating it to what she already knows, and filtering distractions so she can make connections well enough to draw conclusions. Catherine's personal level of stress also influences the degree to which she takes in and interprets information. The frequent reminders her teacher gives her to concentrate, get her work done, and pay attention don't help. Instead, she needs interventions that address these issues.

Interventions That Help with Focus and Attention

Our three students have different attention control problems, but there are strategies that target each area of concern. Let's look at some options that help with the three primary root cause categories: establishing focus, sustaining focus, and transitioning focus.

Establishing Focus

Having attention control problems is like having a camera with a faulty zoom lens. Sometimes students like Catherine zoom in on an unimportant detail when they need the big picture. Sometimes they zoom out and miss important details. Catherine may look like a student who daydreams and is distractible, when in reality she is often just taking a moment to determine what she should be focusing on.

SPOTLIGHT ON PURPOSE. Helping students clearly identify what they need to know by a given time helps them take control of their learning lens. You might say something like, "By the end of this lesson, you should be able to use percentages and fractions to figure out which sales are the best buy" or "By the end of the week, be ready to set up good arguments to convince the electric company to use wind turbines to solve some current problems." Specific learning targets help Catherine filter out unimportant information and zoom in on what is germane.

It is a good idea to double-check how well you have focused students on the goals of the lesson. I often ask at least five students what they need to understand by the end of the class and how this information will be useful in the future. The "what" without the "why" gets surface focus rather than the kind of attention that motivates students to learn important concepts. Even if you tell Catherine what to focus on, her attention will fade quickly if she cannot connect the new ideas to existing knowledge.

CONNECTING NEW INFORMATION TO PRIOR KNOWLEDGE. The more efficiently Catherine's brain sees similarities between the new information and what she already knows, feels, or has experienced, the easier it is for her to control her attention (Anderson, 1998). If she cannot relate to the material, there is little to no chance that her attention will remain focused. Questions like, "How is this like what we studied yesterday?" or "When have you felt the same as this character?" help Catherine connect with her prior knowledge.

Advance organizers that list focusing questions or graphic organizers like KWL charts also help students link the known to the new. KWL charts generally have three columns: the *K* column for listing what students already *know* about a topic; the *W* column for listing what they *want* to know; and the *L* column, where students can summarize what they actually *learned*. Organizers are helpful but hard to use if students have little prior knowledge to connect to. You may need to plan concrete experiences to create the link.

The more abstract the information, the harder it is to sort the important from the unimportant. Starting lessons with a real-life activity can help. For example, before beginning a lesson on area and perimeter, you might ask Catherine to figure out different ways to determine whether the storage cabinet in the back of the room will fit in the space behind your desk. This type of investigation activity builds prior knowledge to support the upcoming abstract work.

Sometimes focus questions and experiences alone don't do the job, and you have to think of another way to hook attention.

SEEING THE PERSONAL IMPORTANCE OF THE LEARNING. "Because it's on the test" only inspires students who care about tests. Grades don't hold much value for Catherine because she seldom gets good grades, except in art class. For her, school is often about demands she cannot meet and things she doesn't see as particularly useful or interesting. In art class, however, Catherine sees learning differently. She experiences an environment that her teacher, Mrs. Watson, purposefully designs to stress relevance. Mrs. Watson makes herself aware of her students' interests and styles and then incorporates activities that she knows her students will find appealing. Mrs. Watson believes in Catherine and shows it by challenging her with rigorous work without pushing so hard that Catherine stresses out and gives up. She constantly points out Catherine's strengths and points out specific and helpful ways for Catherine to increase her success. Building choices into the assignments is another way Mrs. Watson taps into each student's feelings of personal importance.

Appealing to styles and interests, providing useful feedback, and incorporating student choices create a student-centered environment that helps all students focus better. The other part of the focus equation is the ability to block out distractions.

INHIBITING DISTRACTIONS. Your brain is like a scanner constantly searching for novel and interesting things in the environment. With distractions coming in from all directions all the time, it is a wonder we ever stay focused. Even our own thoughts are hard to control. Fortunately, we have neural circuitry designed to help us block urges and intrusive thoughts; unfortunately, this system is shaky at best. You might think of this mental distraction inhibitor as our brain's braking system, and some students' brakes work a lot better than others'.

To pay attention to anything means that students like Catherine and Lance have to apply the brakes to unrelated stimuli. Factors like mental fatigue, boring material, and disruptions make their mental brakes difficult to operate, and the resulting symptoms are missed social cues, crankiness, restlessness, confusion, off-task behavior, and poor decision making. But there are strategies we can use to help their brakes block distractions more efficiently.

Because it takes lots of energy to use the brain's distraction inhibitor, the lower Lance's personal battery, the more poorly his brakes perform. Getting enough sleep is high on the list of interventions, but interspersing work time with short breaks can restore inhibitory chemicals in Lance's brain. This is especially true if the rest period is outdoors. Natural environments have such a positive effect that research (Nauert, 2010) suggests even looking out the window or at pictures of nature can help refresh the brain's attention circuits.

Sustaining Attention

Once you have a student's attention, the big challenge is keeping it. A common obstacle to sustained attention is the length of time a teacher expects the student to concentrate. Generally, students with focusing dysfunctions cannot tolerate long periods of sitting, standing, or passive listening. The more concentration required, the more these students need to move, talk, and be actively engaged to maintain alertness. Active engagement is the student equivalent of the cup of coffee many adults use to get themselves going. How long can students sit passively and listen without interacting?

PACING OF LESSONS. When it comes to passive learning, you can use your students' age as a guide: don't lecture for more minutes than years your students have been alive without stopping to involve them in active reflection or processing activities. I carry a small timer (Logitech wireless presenter) that buzzes like a cell phone to indicate when I should pause in my presentation to let my audience interact. If I have a group of 9-year-olds, I set my timer for nine minutes. It silently vibrates when I have five minutes left to let me know I should start summing up my talk and then gives me a two-minute warning to keep me from giving in to the temptation to drone on and "cover the material" at the expense of student learning.

VARIETY OF STYLES. There is a companion concept that makes the pacing of lessons work: variety in the styles of activities. Lessons that follow a mixed pattern—listen, talk to your partner, listen, draw an example, listen, read and discuss with a partner—followed by a summary are more likely to hold anyone's attention longer than the "listen for what seems like forever and then do independent work" model.

Many adults believe they need to limit stimulation for students with attention problems. This is a good idea when dealing with behavior problems; students like Lance feed on intense emotions and excitement, so you may be pouring gas on burning embers if you lose your cool when disciplining him. However, just the opposite is true for learning situations. Students' attention problems in class are often the result of being understimulated. Students like Lance chronically seek external stimuli to increase their dopamine levels (a neurotransmitter in the brain that causes pleasure and decreases anxiety) so they can muster the energy to focus (Sikström & Söderlund, 2007). The incorporation of white noise, movement, active engagement, and visualization will help students like Lance soak up more information.

- *White noise.* In research conducted by Sikström and Söderlund (2007), students with attention problems were asked to work while listening to various levels of white noise. The findings revealed that the level of background noise that would interfere with most students' performance actually improved performance for students with serious attention problems. The tricky part is determining the exact level of background noise that would enhance a student's ability to focus; it is different for each individual. Better break out those headphones and MP3 players. We also need to consider other forms of external stimulation when music isn't appropriate.

- *Movement.* Some students need fidget toys like squeeze balls or inflated seat cushions to be able to focus, while others do better when they have the option of standing while they work. In my classroom, a podium in the back of the room served as an alternative learning place. Students could choose to learn in a sitting or a standing position as long as they moved quietly. Initially, this corner saw a lot of action, but as the novelty wore off, only the students who really needed it took advantage of the opportunity.
- *Active engagement.* "Active" doesn't necessarily mean moving, wiggling, or walking; it can encompass other forms of student engagement, even talking. Research (Alton-Lee, Nuthall, & Patrick, 1993) shows that students who talk to one another in a focused way and grapple with solving problems learn more deeply than do those who passively listen. Activities that combine movement, discussion, and problem solving are most successful for students like Lance who need help sustaining attention.

    For example, when Miss Meyer saw that interest in reading about the Crusades was waning in her social studies class, she inserted some short but interesting engagement activities into the lessons. First, she had her students demonstrate the basics of sword fighting and jousting. Then, before assigning the Crusades research paper, she asked students to stand on a timeline from the years 1096 to 1272 and guess which of the nine crusades happened during that time. A few days later, she asked a group of students to find and hold things in the room that would be the same weight as a crusader's helmet, shield, sword, and armor. After passing these items around, the students discussed how it must have felt to go to battle carrying that much weight. Helping students grasp concepts in more tangible ways not only focuses their attention but also supports visualization skills that increase memory.
- *Visualization.* This technique increases attention by making movement and feelings more mental than physical. For example, having students visualize what it would feel like to be on a slave ship made Miss Meyer's history lesson come alive for Lance because the mental images were so vivid. Miss Meyer directed the visualization with sensory detail: "Think cramped quarters, maggots crawling on you, the smells of no baths for weeks, and no bathroom of any kind. Feel someone using a whip on your back, which is already screaming in pain from the work of rowing, while your stomach is growling from lack of food."

Using sensory activities that students find engaging colors their emotional brains with strong feelings that increase focus. According to Hebb's Law, "Neurons that fire together, wire together." Just make sure students connect the movement or imaging to the objective for the lesson, or these end up being distractions rather than focusing techniques.

SELF-MONITORING. It is hard to solve problems if you don't know exactly what is causing them. Self-monitoring can help students understand their attention problems so that they can actively work on solutions. Miss Meyer has a plan to teach Lance self-monitoring skills. Each day, Lance picks up a small chart to help him track his own on- and off-task behavior. He wears a small timer during independent work time that vibrates every three minutes. This timer reminds him to check whether he is on or off task and record the data in the appropriate box. If he is off task, he jots down what distracted him. Figure 5.2 shows part of one day's data.

At first, Miss Meyer was concerned that Lance would not be accurate in his assessment of how he was doing, but she recorded her own data on a piece of masking tape she stuck to her arm. Every time she saw Lance go off task, she simply made a check on the tape so she could compare her data with Lance's at the end of the period. As the days and discussions went on, Lance became more aware of exactly what constituted being "off task" and what he should write on his chart.

The charted information guided three changes Lance and Miss Meyer made to his intervention plan. First, they decided that repeating instructions to a partner before starting an assignment would help him make sure he had taken in all the directions, and it would be good practice for the entire class. To address the "problem was too hard" issue, Lance joined three of his classmates who also struggled with reading the social studies material in small-group instruction.

5.2 | Lance's Self-Monitoring Chart for On-Task Behavior

Lance: Feb. 4			
Time period	On task	Off task	Distraction
1		✓	Didn't understand assignment
2	✓		
3		✓	Problem was too hard. I didn't want to do it.
4		✓	Noise in the hallway

As for the noise in the hallway, Lance chose to move his seat away from the door so he would have an easier time concentrating.

Learning to recognize and reduce his own distractions will help Lance throughout his life. For some students, however, the problem isn't focusing or sustaining attention but being so focused that they cannot shift their attention to another idea or activity.

Transitioning Focus

Students with transition problems need to slow down and think through their priorities in order to refocus. The brain doesn't stop on a dime. It may need transition signals like sounds, visual cues, routines, or pictures to redirect thinking. Some students, like Cheree, don't pick up on the subtle or internal signals that most students are aware of when things are about to change. These students need more overt prompts.

REDUCE THE STRESS OF TRANSITIONS. Giving cues is crucial for smooth transitions. Cheree's teacher uses a visual timer to help Cheree see how much time has elapsed. As the red circle disappears, it clearly defines how much time is left so that Cheree can mentally prepare herself to stop her writing assignment and get ready to move on to the next subject. Cues like dropping a card on her desk that says "time to change classes" or "get your textbook out" give Cheree a heads-up about what to expect next.

VISUAL STEPS FOR PLANNING TRANSITIONS. Cheree needs to keep her purpose and the sequence of her tasks in her sight. Visual agendas or "to do" lists help define tasks in order. At first, Cheree could only operate with three things at a time on her list, but now she has as many as six. Cheree checks off each item as she completes it to reward herself.

TRANSFER OF SKILLS TO DIFFERENT SITUATIONS AND ENVIRONMENTS. Cheree is learning to work with a partner during math class, but when asked to do the same thing in science, she cannot remember the routines and responsibilities. Adults cannot afford to leave the ability to apply new skills to novel situations to chance. This "transfer" step must be explicitly taught. To teach the ability to transfer, at first it is important to discuss when and where the new skill will be useful. Then students will need opportunities to practice the strategy in different settings with different problems. For example, Cheree's teacher, Mrs. Barton, decides to use the same guidelines for doing partner work in each subject area. She has students help her create a poster listing the four rules of working with a partner, and they discuss how these rules will help everyone learn more efficiently. Each day before doing partner work, the class members review at least one rule and talk about how they might need to adjust as various situations arise.

Root Causes of Poor Reading Comprehension

Attention control is important to learning in all subjects, but when a student is reading, that control is the difference between word calling and comprehending. Many students who have executive dysfunction related to focusing attention also have trouble reading, which requires focus on purpose, sustained attention, and ability to switch focus. Our three case study students all have noted difficulty with reading. As always with problem solving, finding a specific reason for the trouble is the key. Use Figure 5.3 (p. 110) to help you identify possible root causes of poor reading comprehension. Do you spot anything that may factor in the reading problems Catherine, Cheree, and Lance are having?

Catherine's problem with comprehension and responding appropriately to assignments appears to be a combination of lack of focus on a clear purpose, inability to see relevance, and overlooking critical details as she reads. Catherine's teachers know that her long history of failure has taken its toll on her confidence and increased her stress levels. They will design an action plan that gives Catherine new tools for keeping herself focused on both her purpose and real-world applications for reading. Strategies that emphasize helpful feedback, vocabulary expansion, and connection of concepts through active engagement will be high on the priority list.

Lance's teachers have decided that his drifting attention is a result of his inability to filter distracting information so that he can identify key ideas. He also needs a lot of work on creating mental pictures as he reads to help him become aware of patterns. His action plan will include working on retelling skills that require synthesizing and summarizing information so he can solve problems and draw logical conclusions.

Cheree's lack of fluency skills (phrase reading, expression, and attention to punctuation) is interfering with her ability to make sense of what she reads. The fact that she keeps on reading even when her errors cause the text not to make sense worries her teachers. Cheree's action plan will include repeated reading strategies to increase her fluency and retelling skills to help her self-monitor as she reads.

5.3 | Root Causes of Poor Reading Comprehension

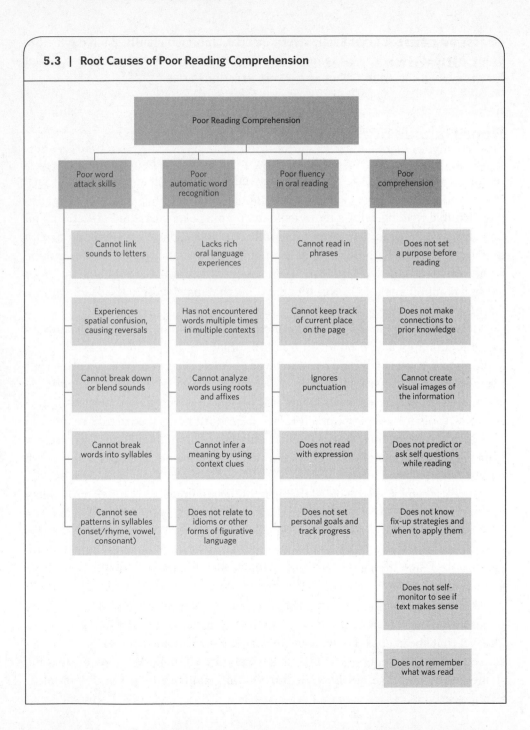

Interventions for Students with Poor Reading Comprehension

Reading can seem like an insurmountable task for students with attention difficulties. In order to comprehend, they must focus on the purpose, pay attention to the words, and make connections with the text all at the same time—not an easy task when your mental steering and braking system is faulty. Sometimes reading is so frustrating that these students just stop trying. To keep stress levels down and motivation up, teachers should break difficult reading tasks down into small steps, include lots of variety, and plan mental breaks. Here are some techniques to support attention during reading.

Finding the Main Idea

Catherine and Lance sound like they are reading fluently, but because of their erratic and unfocused attention, they have a hard time connecting what they are reading to what they already know. Because they aren't focused on a specific purpose, by the end of the page they don't have a clue what they just read.

Lance needs to filter out not only unimportant information but also the giggling behind him, the paper wad flying over him, and the buzz coming in from the hallway to his right. Focusing on too many things at once causes clutter in the head, so what Lance needs is a way to dig out the main ideas of his reading from the avalanche of information pouring down on him. He needs a "mental spotlight" shining on what he should be looking for. Lance's reading specialist, Mrs. Jenkins, has a set of strategies for helping him zoom in on a few main ideas.

Mrs. Jenkins starts by asking Lance to highlight only the important parts of a one-page text. Lance's page ends up being almost entirely yellow, so Mrs. Jenkins asks him to limit his highlighting to no more than 10 words or phrases in each paragraph. When he is finished, Mrs. Jenkins sees that his highlighting is pretty random, so she asks Lance to explain why he chose the words he did. When he is unable to explain, Mrs. Jenkins decides to teach Lance five steps for identifying main ideas and key details:

1. **Find the topic.** Students first need to know that it usually takes a couple of read-throughs to find a text's main idea: one read to find out what the whole passage is about and then a second to see if the topic selected is

the right one. After explaining this to Lance, Mrs. Jenkins reads the selected passage aloud:

> Metamorphic rock makes up about 85 percent of the deep continental crust of the earth. It is formed when rocks that already exist deep beneath the surface change due to intense heat and pressure. Some of the heat that forms this rock comes from magma or molten rock. This rock forms from pressure that comes from being squeezed by the heavy layers of rock above it. Over a few million years, the original rock partially melts, causing some of the chemicals to rearrange themselves and form the new type of rock.

She reports to Lance, "After my first read, I see that the word *rock* keeps coming up, specifically the term *metamorphic rock.*"

2. **Double-check.** The next step is to review the topic selection. Mrs. Jenkins tells Lance, "Now I am going to double-check that *rock* is really the key idea by placing a check mark next to each sentence that has anything to do with metamorphic rock." Seeing that every sentence is marked by a check, Mrs. Jenkins and Lance are satisfied that she has found the main topic.

3. **Highlight keywords and key phrases.** Next, Mrs. Jenkins shows Lance how she uses the topic of metamorphic rock to find and highlight the keywords and key phrases. She then makes a list of these words. She points out that she doesn't record sentences in her list, only words and phrases. Here are the ones she chooses: *deep in the earth, heat, pressure, magma, squeezed, millions of years, partially melts, chemicals change,* and *new rock.*

4. **Synthesize with graphic organizer.** Once the student has the keywords and key phrases, fitting them together is the challenge. A graphic organizer is a useful way for students to synthesize this information. Mrs. Jenkins shows Lance how to use a web to connect words from her list. She explains as she works: "I might add a few new words or drop some from my list as I organize my thoughts. This web will help me remember all the important ideas without having to do too much writing. Sometimes I like taking notes this way instead of using an outline." Figure 5.4 shows the web she creates.

5. **Summarize orally.** Whereas synthesizing is noting what is important, summarizing is describing what you've learned in a succinct way. After Mrs. Jenkins helps Lance use a web to synthesize his own text, she has him summarize orally using only his web. Lance is amazed at how easy

5.4 | Sample Web for Synthesizing Information

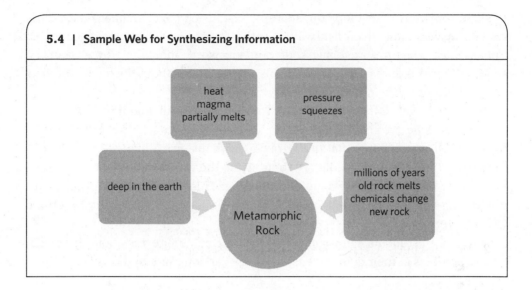

it is to remember the information. Mrs. Jenkins knows that this active processing skill will help, but only after they have practiced together multiple times.

Summarizing is an essential comprehension skill, but it will work only if Lance has some frame of reference that helps him understand what he is reading.

Creating Mental Pictures

What helps us enjoy reading is our ability to translate words on a page into pictures in our heads. Our personal pictures tend to be more satisfying than someone else's interpretation of the story. How often have you heard someone criticize a movie by comparing it with the book version with a comment like "That movie was a disappointment. I didn't envision that character as such a pretty boy. He should have been tall, dark, and rugged"? Students who read without making mental pictures lose comprehension as well as the satisfaction of creating their personalized version of the text.

To help Lance with comprehension and encourage her other students to strengthen their visualization skills, Mrs. Cooper decides to read aloud to them without showing any of the text's illustrations. She gives the students whiteboards to sketch their own mental pictures as she reads each page. Initially, Lance finds visualizing very difficult, until he watches other students and listens to their ideas. Unlike Lance, who loves sketching, some students worry about their drawing ability, so Mrs. Cooper assures everyone that this activity is not about the quality of their art, just capturing their mental pictures.

After each page, Mrs. Cooper stops to let students talk about what they saw in their heads before she has them compare their pictures with what the illustrator drew. She emphasizes that their drawings are just as valuable as the illustrator's depictions because reading is about using the words of the text to create a vision that helps you understand the meaning. This strategy is a turning point for Lance, who said he didn't know he was supposed to make mental pictures when he reads.

Even when students can visualize what they think the text is about, there can be gaping holes in their comprehension if they cannot relate to the vocabulary.

Working on Vocabulary

Rich and varied vocabulary provides background knowledge and is critical to comprehension and achievement (National Institute of Child Health and Human Development, 2000). If students do not grasp 98 percent of the words read, they generally have difficulty getting a deep understanding of the content (Hseuh-chao & Nation, 2000). Catherine's English teacher, Mr. DeLauter, knows vocabulary is more than just memorizing the definitions of a list of words. He makes sure his students understand multiple meanings and how words link to other words, and he uses a variety of techniques to actively engage and focus their attention.

Unfortunately, most teachers don't spend nearly enough time on direct teaching of vocabulary, so Mr. DeLauter has been asked to share the strategies he uses in his English class with teachers in the other departments. This helps students transfer the skills they learn in English class to unfamiliar territory. The staff is becoming aware of the fact that the higher the grade, the more essential it is to purposefully teach vocabulary. Let's take a look at some particularly effective strategies.

ELABORATIVE REHEARSAL. *Elaborative rehearsal* refers to deep processing of what is to be remembered. A great tool for elaborative rehearsal is the Frayer model (Frayer, Frederick, & Klausmeier, 1969), which uses a graphic organizer to define a word in multiple ways, both linguistically and nonlinguistically. In the middle of the organizer is the vocabulary word. The upper left-hand corner contains the word's definition, and the upper right-hand corner contains characteristics or facts. The

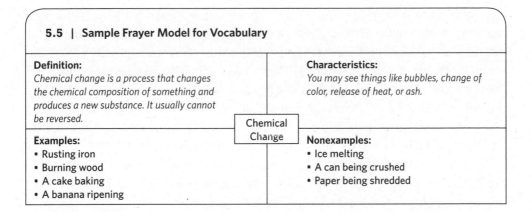

5.5 | Sample Frayer Model for Vocabulary

Definition:	Characteristics:
Chemical change is a process that changes the chemical composition of something and produces a new substance. It usually cannot be reversed.	*You may see things like bubbles, change of color, release of heat, or ash.*

Chemical Change

Examples:	Nonexamples:
• Rusting iron • Burning wood • A cake baking • A banana ripening	• Ice melting • A can being crushed • Paper being shredded

lower left-hand corner gives examples, such as drawings or a sentence containing the word, while the lower right-hand corner contains nonexamples, like antonyms or pictures and words that do not fit the category of the vocabulary word.

Mr. DeLauter encouraged Catherine to use a Frayer model in every subject to make mental connections for tough concepts. Figure 5.5 is an example of one of his model cards that he helped Catherine apply to her science lesson.

Once the frame is developed, Mr. DeLauter sometimes uses the model backward. All the information is complete, but the keyword is missing, and Catherine has to deduce the word. Visit http://wvde.state.wv.us/strategybank/FrayerModel.html for help with creating these models.

FIGURATIVE LANGUAGE FUN. Idioms are expressions that have hidden meanings, like "hold your horses" or "letting the cat out of the bag." You cannot predict the meaning of an idiom from the typical meanings of the individual words in the phrase or expression. Idioms are embedded in our everyday language and can be confusing to students who are unfamiliar with these expressions. Deciphering these phrases is especially hard for students who are learning to communicate in a second language and for those who are already struggling with comprehension problems. Fortunately, there is a lot of fun to be had with idioms, which helps hold the attention of less focused students.

To teach her elementary students about idioms, Mrs. Cooper had them read *Amelia Bedelia* by Peggy Parish or *In a Pickle and Other Funny Idioms* by Marvin Terban and Giulio Maestro. They discussed why these books are only fun when you understand both the literal and figurative meanings of the idioms in the book.

Next, the students went to an interactive game called "Eye on Idioms," found on the ReadWriteThink website (http://www.readwritethink.org) under the listing for interactive classroom resources. The activity showed drawings that depicted the literal meanings of idioms, and the students had to choose the matching idiom and guess the figurative meaning. Mrs. Cooper's students then paired up to create their own idiom guessing game. One student either drew or developed a skit showing the literal meaning of an idiom while his or her partner illustrated, wrote an explanation of, or made a plan for acting out the figurative meaning.

A good grounding in vocabulary is essential for success in school, but if you do not have automatic and fluid recognition of that vocabulary, your lack of fluency will destroy your comprehension.

Increasing Fluency

Students who struggle with sustaining attention often have difficulty with fluency. Reading with expression and attending to punctuation allow meaning to emerge. Mrs. Barton is using several fluency interventions to help Cheree with her lack of comprehension.

Second grade is tough for Cheree because of her difficulty in reading. Although she can sound out words in isolation, she lumbers along word by word as she reads and simply blows by the punctuation as if it weren't there. She totally lacks any sense of phrasing or expression. This poor fluency makes focusing attention even harder and therefore scuttles Cheree's reading comprehension.

When readers use all their mental energy identifying each word, they can't focus enough to make connections among ideas within the text or with their own prior knowledge. To master reading fluency, Cheree needs lots of practice on automatic word and phrase recognition so she can read with enough expression to make the text understandable. Research shows that repeated oral reading practice is far superior to silent independent reading for improving fluency (Hasbrouck & Tindal, 2005). Here are a few techniques Mrs. Barton uses.

ECHO-READING. A text selection with 50–200 words works best for the echo-reading strategy. The teacher starts by reading a sentence from the text, and then the student repeats the same sentence alone using the same expression and phrasing. At first, Cheree could only imitate reading short phrases after Mrs. Barton read, but now she is comfortable with whole sentences. Sometimes, after Cheree and Mrs. Barton have practiced a selection three or four times, Cheree asks to read by herself. Soon Cheree will be able to listen to several sentences before echoing what she hears. The keys to her success are short sessions (about 10 minutes long) and lots of positive feedback from Mrs. Barton to keep Cheree's motivation high.

RADIO READS. There is something about reading a passage over and over that can put kids' brains into a coma. A fun way to change it up is to have students read and perform from a script. Once Mrs. Barton's students knew they had a certain part to read in the "radio reading" broadcast, they were more than willing to practice the same material repeatedly to get their parts right for the performance. They were especially excited when they were encouraged to add sound effects and record their broadcast.

Knowing and Using Reading Strategies Appropriately

Poor readers are often unaware when their comprehension breaks down, and some don't know what to do when they do notice that the text doesn't make sense. For students to select and use reading strategies flexibly, teachers need to model the strategies, provide scheduled oral practice, and give corrective feedback (Honig, Diamond, & Gutlohn, 2008). As students verbalize their thinking, the teacher will be able to catch their errors and redirect them. Mrs. Barton uses partner reading as the research-based approach to introduce and practice these strategies (Fuchs, Fuchs, & Burish, 2000).

CUE CARDS. Have students write out a key question to focus their purpose for reading and use it as a bookmark. For example, the cue card could ask, "Why was there a dispute about whether or not the United States should enter into the war?" or "Who in this story would be a good friend for you, and why?" Before reading each page, they should use the cue card to remind themselves of what information they should be looking for.

RETELLING. Many students with focusing problems have a hard time "connecting the dots" as they read. As a result, they just keep reading even when the text doesn't make sense to them. They completely miss things that would help them make sense of the material, like patterns in the sequence of the plot, character development, the structure of the writing, and clues for drawing valid inferences. Retelling increases students' ability to listen to what they are reading or hearing and then summarize a deeper-than-literal understanding of the key ideas in their own words.

In her 2nd grade class, Mrs. Barton generally starts teaching this skill by using short books that include predictable patterns and just a few characters. She focuses students before they start reading by saying, "When we are finished with this story, I am going to ask you this question: 'What happened in the beginning, in the middle, and at the end of the story?' Are you ready?"

Mrs. Barton stops after a few pages and asks, "Who can tell me what has happened so far, in the beginning of our story? Remember to use just a few words, and tell me only the most important parts. Good. Now what do you think might happen next?" She repeats this type of questioning in the middle and at the end of the story. Mrs. Barton then asks the students to close their eyes and play a movie in their head showing all three parts of the story before doing their big retell. She sometimes has students act out the story, draw three pictures depicting the three parts, or videotape themselves explaining what happens in the book in enough detail that a person who has not read the book can understand it.

More complex retellings require students to explain the causes of events and motivations behind characters' actions or to evaluate the text. In her 5th grade class, Mrs. Cooper uses checklists or webs to help students visualize and reconstruct story structures. For example, she asked Lance to show the four ways the author developed his character (through description of her appearance, what she said, what she did, and what other characters in the story said about her). This retelling required more than simple recall; it prompted Lance to dig for deeper understandings that enabled him to draw conclusions about what type of person this character really was and accurately predict how she would act and react.

STICKY-NOTE STRATEGY. One strategy that keeps students more aware of how well they are maintaining focus and making sense of what they read is the sticky-note strategy. This exercise requires students to react to the text by writing or drawing responses on sticky notes that they attach to the margins as they read. The type of responses change according to the purpose of the reading and whether the text is fiction or nonfiction.

For example, when reading fiction, Catherine may be asked to stop two or three times on each page to jot down questions like "What just happened? What will happen next? What does that word mean? Why did that character do that? What does this remind me of?"

When reading nonfiction text, the sticky-note responses would change to questions like "What is the key idea? What five facts support that idea? How is this like something I know? How does this passage relate to the main idea? How can I use this information? What does that word mean? What confuses me? Do I agree with this?"

Because the sticky-note questions are selected to focus on a specific purpose, the active reading process becomes less intimidating and more engaging. The notes help Catherine hold on to her thoughts as she reads and give her a record to launch her next steps of reporting on the reading, participating in class, or organizing a written response.

Five-Step Problem-Solving Case Study: Poor Focus and Reading Comprehension

Students with attention problems exhibit a range of behaviors, from fidgety and talkative (like our friend Lance) to quiet and lost in their own world (Catherine). Digging under what is often seen as undisciplined or uninterested behavior to the root causes of focus issues can make a big difference in student success and lead to improvement in related reading problems. Few skills are more important to academic learning than reading comprehension. As with focus issues, signs of comprehension problems vary widely, from obviously halting, word-by-word reading to perfect word calling with zero understanding. Let's meet our case study student, Tina, and see what we can uncover about her behavior in class and her difficulty with reading.

> *Tina is a quiet but congenial 4th grade student who is new to the school this year. Mr. Burns is worried about her because when called on, she sits and stares as if she didn't hear the question. When he asks, she says she hears him, but there is typically a big delay before she answers. Mr. Burns has also noticed that when Tina comes to a word she doesn't know, she stops in her tracks. She doesn't seem to have strategies for figuring out problems that are difficult for her. She simply stops working.*

Mr. Burns is confused about what to do for Tina. He sets up a meeting to consult with Mrs. Apolito, the special education teacher who has been trained as a problem-solving coach.

Step 1. Know the Student

Mrs. Apolito has Mr. Burns make a list (see Figure 5.6, p. 120) of his concerns about Tina's academic progress and classroom behavior. At the top of this list are "poor comprehension" and "daydreams." He also includes some of Tina's strengths, like "wants to please the teacher."

5.6 | Strengths and Concerns Chart for Tina

Name: Tina Wampler
Grade: 4

Academic concerns:	Behavior concerns:
• Poor comprehension • No phonic skills • Finds writing difficult • Poor spelling • Weak problem-solving skills	• Daydreams and loses her place while working • Seldom completes her work—15% completion • Withdrawn, doesn't volunteer in class • When called on, she just sits there and doesn't answer

Strengths to build on:	
• Good speaking vocabulary • Has traveled extensively • Good storyteller	• Wants to please the teacher • Reads at beginning 2nd grade level • Quick at math facts

Step 2. Analyze the Root Causes

Mr. Burns and the coach use the list and the flowcharts for analyzing root causes of attention problems (Figure 5.1) and reading comprehension problems (Figure 5.3) as they talk about Tina. They will involve the school reading specialist, Mrs. Jenkins, in their problem-solving process later on, but the first conversation is just between Mr. Burns and Mrs. Apolito, the coach. Let's see what they are able to discover about Tina's behavior.

Coach: Why do you think Tina is having such a hard time?

Mr. Burns: She has moved a lot, but I think it's mostly her reading problem that is catching up to her this year. There is so much reading now, and she plods along with minimal comprehension.

Coach: What is causing that comprehension problem, in your opinion?

Mr. Burns: Any number of the causes on the reading flowchart [Figure 5.3] seem to fit. I don't see her using any word attack skills, and she can't read in phrases. Her word-by-word reading destroys her comprehension. I don't know if her "lost in space" look is because she can't read or if it is a more pervasive focusing problem. I'm thinking focusing, though, because I lose her during lectures, too.

Coach: OK, so we have phonics, focusing issues, fluency, and comprehension problems.

Mr. Burns: Yes, I've talked to Mrs. Jenkins about doing a reading assessment. Maybe we should concentrate on helping her survive academically by providing partners and technology to support the reading until Mrs. Jenkins can help us. Meanwhile, we can tackle the attention problems.

Coach: Perfect. So what causes Tina's lack of focus?

Mr. Burns: Other than the difficulty of the work? I think she drifts off and forgets what she is supposed to do.

Coach: And what causes the drifting?

Mr. Burns: Looking at the attention chart [Figure 5.1], I would say that she may not get the goal of the lesson or the instructions in the first place, and I doubt that she self-monitors well enough to know when she is off track.

Coach: That sounds like a great place to start. So do you think our focus for the next four weeks should be helping Tina set clear goals for her work and self-monitor how well she stays with those goals?

Mr. Burns: Yes, and then we will add the reading interventions next week.

Step 3. Set a Clear and Measurable Goal

Because they are tackling Tina's focus and reading problems in two stages, Mr. Burns and the coach set two goals. They start with what they predict will be the outcome of their attention control work with Tina and select a goal for that:

> **Hypothesis:** If we teach Tina focusing and self-monitoring skills, she will pay attention in class and finish more work.
>
> **Time frame and measurement benchmarks:** Within five weeks, Tina will be able to state her goal when working and will go from completing 15 percent of her work to at least 50 percent.

When Mr. Burns and the coach are able to meet with Mrs. Jenkins, the reading specialist, they agree on a goal for skill improvement:

> **Hypothesis:** If we teach Tina beginning and ending sounds as well as fluency skills, she will comprehend better and finish more work.
>
> **Time frame and measurement benchmarks:** Within eight weeks, her fluency score will go from 72 words correct per minute (wcpm) to 95 wcpm. Her work completion will go from 15 to 50 percent.

Mrs. Jenkins set two measurable goals for Tina's reading: one for fluency and one for work completion. Notice that the team doesn't expect improvement overnight. Supporting students with executive delays takes patient and consistent instruction over the long haul.

Step 4. Decide How to Monitor Student Progress

Mr. Burns taught Tina to ask herself, "What am I thinking about right now?" and "What should I be paying attention to?" He gave Tina a headset and a recording of a tape that chimed every minute during independent work time. (This time interval gradually faded to every four minutes over a period of three weeks and then went to an intermittent chime). Tina used the school's on-task behavior form (like the one in Figure 5.2) to self-monitor. Every time Tina heard the chime, she recorded whether she was on task or not, but at this point she was not asked to record what distracted her.

During the first week, an aide came to the room for 20 minutes daily and also kept a record of Tina's on-task time, comparing her data with Tina's record. After the adults were certain Tina understood exactly what to look for and record, Mr. Burns took over tracking intermittently throughout the period and then conferenced with Tina.

To chart and reflect on Tina's reading progress, Mrs. Jenkins used an oral fluency growth chart (see Figure 5.7). Each week, Tina read for one minute from a passage at her projected reading level for the end of the year while Mrs. Jenkins kept track of Tina's errors. At the end of the time, they subtracted Tina's errors from the total number of words read and plotted her score on the chart. Because this technique tracks progress in such small units, it is easy for Tina to see that she is exceeding the projected growth of the goal. She is over-the-moon happy about her growth. Actually seeing her progress on a visual chart is changing Tina's whole attitude about her ability to learn to read.

Step 5. Select an Action Plan from a List of Options

Tina's team selects interventions that they think match the root causes of her problems, and they put together an action plan (see Figure 5.8, p. 124) that lists strategies for teachers, for Tina, and for her parents to use to build her skills.

5.7 | Tina's Self-Monitoring Chart for Oral Fluency

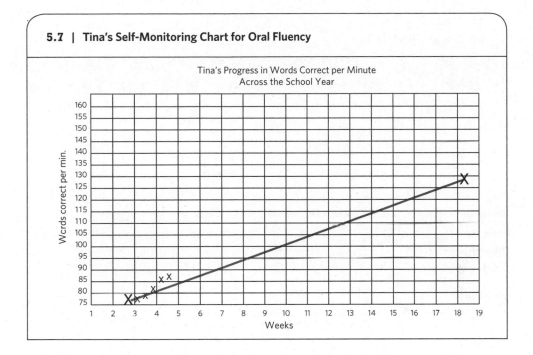

Tina's Progress in Words Correct per Minute
Across the School Year

Because Tina has such a hard time learning phonics, Mrs. Jenkins recommends using the neurological impress method (Flood, Lapp, & Fisher, 2005) as the initial approach to increasing Tina's reading fluency. This method has shown significant results with students of all ages in a short amount of time, and Tina desperately needs a quick boost in confidence. Here is the protocol for the neurological impress method:

- *Allow the student to select* from a variety of passages. Poems, songs, and predictable stories tend to be the most fun and are easiest for most students to start with.
- *Sit in a comfortable and relaxed position* to the right of the student so your voice can be close to the student's ear.
- *As you and the student read in unison,* raise your voice a little louder than the student's during difficult passages and get softer when the student is doing well. Chunk reading into phrases, pause for punctuation, use careful articulation, and go for enthusiasm.
- *To train the student's eyes to flow across the page,* move your finger in a smooth continuous manner, matching the precise speed of the verbal reading.

5.8 | Action Plan for Tina

Skills Needed	Teaching Strategies	Student Responsibilities	Suggestions for Parents
Focusing before reading	• After telling Tina the purpose of the lesson, ask her to restate it sometime during the lesson (all teachers). • Teachers will provide advance organizers to help Tina focus on key issues. • When Tina stalls out and doesn't answer, remind her to say, "I will answer you in just a minute."	• Make yourself a cue card to help you remember what to pay attention to (all classrooms).	• After giving Tina a task or chore with two-step instructions, ask her to repeat the instructions, and then check back to see if she can repeat them again in five minutes.
Phrase-reading and stopping for punctuation	• Use the neurological impress method in the reading lab 5–10 minutes daily for 8 weeks.	• After your partner reading, read the passage (classroom).	• For five minutes a night, use neurological impress followed by a short retell.
Beginning and ending sounds	• Provide structured phonics instruction in the reading lab, focusing on beginning and ending sounds at first.	• Group picture cards by their beginning and ending sounds. Self-check is on the backs of the cards (lab).	• If Tina gets stuck on a word, just tell her what it is, have her repeat it, and go on.
Comprehension	• Use small-group instruction to model one strategy a day, followed by partner reading for practice using the same strategy. The main strategy for week one is retelling. • Teach the sticky-note strategy to focus on key ideas. • Every teacher will ask Tina to summarize one thing she learned each day.	• Make a list of strategies and keep track of how many times you use them in science class. • Start with retelling. You will use sticky notes to write key words to help you remember what you read.	• Watch the video of Tina and her teacher using the daily strategies and practice one each night after the neurological impress reading session, using her regular homework as the reading material (no more than five minutes). • Ask Tina to describe one thing she learned each day.

At the end of a line, move your finger rapidly back to the beginning of the next line. Help the student gradually take over the tracking.

- *Do not stop, ask questions, or correct the student* during reading. This is about getting the automatic flow of written language. You may reread a line, page, or section of a book repeatedly to build fluency.
- *After 5 to 10 minutes of reading, compliment the student* to reinforce his or her effort and things that are done well. After the student is comfortable with the process, you can use an audio version of a reading passage for the student's practice.

Mrs. Jenkins plans to add instruction on reading strategies to strengthen Tina's comprehension and realizes that these skills will not transfer to classroom settings unless all adults reinforce the strategies in the classroom. All teachers are going to start with a simple retelling in each class of one thing Tina reads or hears to keep her focused on basics.

Each classroom teacher will also provide focusing support by asking Tina intermittently to restate the purpose of her work and by providing graphic organizers. Mr. Burns will co-plan with Mrs. Jenkins to establish which reading strategies to emphasize each week. The skills selected will be good practice for the whole class, so he will work this into his lesson plans.

Large-Group Application

Mr. Burns is aware that many of the interventions that work for struggling students can be adapted for the entire class. For instance, he now takes special care to clarify the purpose of each lesson and assignment. Since he started checking on students' understanding of why they are doing the assigned work, he has noticed a new level of cooperation and motivation.

Mr. Burns is also more aware of how he paces instruction. He used to spend too much time talking without interspersing student interaction time for reflection and focusing. Now he plans partner turn-and-talks several times a day to provide oral rehearsals of key concepts. He also uses a "checking buddy" system in which students provide feedback to each other on whether they understand directions or have the correct notes.

Mr. Burns also knows that high engagement increases focus, so he teaches students to have productive conversations by assigning each student in a foursome a specific role. The first student reads the question from the board and puts the question in his or her own words, the second student answers the question, the third student adds something to that answer, and the fourth student summarizes the group's answer and either writes or reports it orally to another group. Students switch responsibilities for each question.

Sometimes Mr. Burns helps focus student attention by coupling discussion with movement. One way he does this is by using a strategy called "four corners." Mr. Burns links corners of the room with choices like "How would you prefer to spend your free time: reading (front right corner); playing sports (back right corner); listening to music (back left corner); or working on your hobby (front left corner)?" This is a forced choice, so students must choose only one designated corner of the room to stand in. Once they are in place, Mr. Burns poses a discussion question related to the topic, each corner group reports out, and students go back to their seats. Students have only 20 seconds to get to their corners and 20 seconds to return to their seats after the discussion. Mr. Burns knows how to build relationships with his students while still enforcing clear guidelines for behavior, which enables him to avoid losing instructional time as he provides a variety of ways and places to learn.

Although Mr. Burns needs to touch base or conference with Tina once or twice a period, it doesn't cause a problem because he stopped doing whole-class instruction for the entire period years ago. He uses at least half of his daily instructional time for paired reading, small-group instruction, collaborative group work, or independent practice. This gives him time to assess and conference with individuals or groups as well as conduct small-group instruction for students who need more modeling and guided practice.

Summary

Students with attention issues can be challenging to work with. They exhibit a variety of symptoms, like being hypersensitive or insensitive, distractible, bored, rigid, frustrated, or "spaced out," to name a few. At times, the spaced-out symptom is simply students' way of shifting to a new mental gear. Unfortunately, the new gear they are supposed to be shifting to is often unclear to them. Students with attention problems need help getting their "mental spotlights" to shine on key ideas and procedures. Their erratic and unfocused attention makes it hard for them to connect new information to what they already know and affects their reading comprehension. For example, they often sound like they are reading fluently, but because they don't focus on a specific purpose for reading, they cannot make the connections for comprehension. Consequently, by the time they reach the end of the page, they don't have a clue about what they just read.

WHAT WORKS: Using direct conversation and cueing to draw attention to what's important; keeping the objective in students' sight because they forget it; using visualization, pictures, and graphic organizers to help students connect to prior knowledge; helping sustain attention by using movement, color, and gamelike activities to vary pace and add variety; directly teaching vocabulary and word attack skills; working on building fluency in reading to support comprehension; listening to students read and explain how they are applying strategies; teaching students ways to self-monitor their on-task behavior as well as their comprehension of reading.

WHAT DOESN'T WORK: Giving long lectures and assignments without breaks; not using variety in approaches; not providing student interaction; assuming that if the student knows the definition of a word he or she understands it; thinking that if the student can read fast he or she comprehends the material; chastising students for not paying attention or forgetting the instructions; forcing the student to read aloud in front of peers who read much better; overloading students on independent worksheets; rushing through material.

In this chapter, we looked at strategies that make it easier for students to succeed by helping them learn to focus and sustain attention, especially while reading. In the next chapter, we will investigate how teachers can manage their classrooms in a way that requires students to step up to the plate and take responsibility for their learning.

On Your Own

Now it's your turn to try using the five-step method to solve the attention and reading problems of our case study student, Gerald.

Case study. *Gerald is a likeable student who would rather play on the computer than read or do worksheets. Wait, that makes him normal, doesn't it? Yes, except for the fact that he struggles with reading because his speaking, listening, and reading vocabulary is about half that of the other students in the classroom. He seldom can repeat directions because he is generally talking to the person next to him or playing with something in his desk.*

IMPULSE CONTROL AND SELF-MONITORING: DEALING WITH DISRUPTIVE BEHAVIOR

Mr. Zornes couldn't believe what he was seeing in his classroom. Scott decided to turn off the Bunsen burner by yanking the hose off the gas nozzle. What in the world was he thinking—again! Flames shot in all directions from the open gas tap. The smell of Scott's singed hair filled the room as a student standing nearby turned off the tap. Scott's behavior is predictable. The resident mad scientist, he never listens during directions and seldom follows them even when he knows what he is supposed to do. He habitually acts first, thinks later.

Melissa is an intelligent student who frequently makes announcements like "This work is pointless, so why do we have to do this garbage?" as she taps her pencil on the desk. She refuses to do homework. Melissa is a master at pushing teachers' buttons by arguing and challenging their authority, and she basks in the attention as 25 pairs of eyes watch her do it. This is a girl with a high desire for power and control who, when asked why she reacts the way she does, isn't sure she has an answer that makes sense even to herself.

Melissa is just the touch of rocket fuel Derek needs to send him straight into orbit. Derek shouts out answers and cracks jokes constantly and is totally unaware when he has gone too far. If someone cuts in front of him in line, a shoving match is bound to follow. When he is unhappy about not being the lab group leader, there is a predictable outburst of temper followed by genuine confusion about why he is in the principal's office. Derek is a good-hearted, fun-loving student who goes with the first thing that comes into his head and rarely can anticipate the consequences of his actions.

The students in this junior high class seem to be in constant competition for the "who can make the poorest choices" award. How can Mr. Zornes run a student-centered classroom when more than half of his 4th-period pupils are out of control? The group has the kind of chemistry that makes science teachers think about ingesting chemicals themselves. Mr. Zornes believes that once he teaches these students to manage their strong feelings and reactions, they have the potential to be his most creative and insightful class. Right now, however, he is wondering how he will ever get these students to work in groups when getting them to work independently is tricky. He wonders how long he can stay the course before some-one yells, "Take Mr. Zornes to the asylum! He's gone off the deep end." He is going to have to provide the kind of structure and guidance that will be as much about teaching self-discipline as science.

We know that when students feel discouraged, bored, left out, or mistreated, they are likely to learn less and misbehave more. If you add in weak executive functioning, the problems are compounded. With a class like this, some teachers unknowingly escalate difficult situations by taking a punishing hard line or with-holding rewards. We call this operating from "position power." The typical result is temporary compliance with escalated student stress and, in some cases, student retaliation waiting in the wings. Not good for anyone.

Teachers like Mr. Zornes who operate from "personal power" are masters at spotting causes beneath the impulsive behaviors that trigger discipline problems. They recognize that blaming or criticizing students or their parents is counter-productive. These master teachers help students develop self-management skills as well as respect for themselves and others. They know how to redirect and guide students without talking too much. They rarely need to send kids to the office, but they do impose consequences for poor choices. These teachers don't operate with "my way or the highway" thinking, nor do they abdicate their responsibility to teach self-control, respect, and responsibility. Teachers who have personal power respond with caring and skill. So what is their secret for managing classrooms with impulsive students? Understanding how the brain works and addressing problems at their roots are the first steps.

Root Causes of Impulsiveness and Weak Self-Monitoring

When the amygdala in our limbic system (the part of our brain that controls emotions) senses a real or perceived threat, it seizes control of our neural energy and limits rational thinking. This is what neurologists refer to as "downshifting" or "emotional hijacking" (Goleman, 1995). When this hijacking occurs, it causes our brain to go into fight (confrontation), flight (avoidance), or freeze (deer in head-lights) mode. When you are in physical danger, these responses can save your life. When the threat is emotional, hijacking forces your brain to make decisions quickly without complete information and reasoning capability.

You have probably experienced the effects of emotional hijacking when you decided not to return a phone call because you wanted to avoid facing the music (flight). Maybe you fired off a scathing text message and then wished for a "retrieve" button on your phone (fight), or during a disagreement you found yourself at a loss for words but hours later came up with several snappy retorts (freeze). The extent to which your thinking brain is compromised depends on the degree of the emotional hijacking.

When the emotional part of your brain is stimulated, it triggers a flood of chemicals, and impulsive behavior results. If the rational part of your brain can stop the flood early, you break the hijack cycle, the chemicals begin to dissipate within three to six seconds, and the thinking and emotional parts of your brain can again work together. If you do not stop the flood, the chemical overdose becomes concentrated, and your brain hurtles you into using your default behaviors for handling stress (cry, punch, run, scream), which may be totally irrational. It will now take about 20 minutes before you can calm yourself enough to have an intelligent conversation or deal with your feelings in a more helpful way (Project EXSEL, 2004).

Self-awareness accompanied by reflective and calming self-talk is the primary way to take control of yourself. Listening to your body's signals, identifying what is really going on, and then managing your emotions is what Daniel Goleman calls *emotional intelligence.* Having the ability to diagnose causes of weaknesses in emotional intelligence is essential for helping students handle upsetting situations.

So what causes students to yell, daydream, shut down, lash out, or play when they should be working? The reasons listed in Figure 6.1 (p. 132), alone or in combination, account for most discipline problems.

Teachers know that Scott needs help internalizing rules and procedures. He can recite what he needs to do but forgets during implementation. More structure, routine, and modeling will help. Scott's blurting problem results from his getting caught up in the excitement of getting attention for entertaining friends as well as from his need for a high level of stimulation to stay focused. Scott needs help slowing himself down and thinking before he reacts. The teachers will work on self-calming and self-monitoring skills to help Scott learn to redirect his own behavior and increase his awareness of how his actions are affecting others. Scott, Derek, and Melissa all have difficulty noticing and interpreting other people's body language accurately and adjusting their responses appropriately.

Melissa's surly attitude is partially due to her tendency to put a negative spin on what people say and do. Her out-of-control home life makes her determined to gain power over her world at school, but she has not figured out how to do this in a positive way. She needs help learning to accurately articulate her feelings and use self-calming techniques to help her manage her anxieties. Reframing strategies will also give her new tools to cope with her stress without avoiding difficult situations or wallowing in self-pity. Once Melissa can identify what triggers her aggressive responses, she will have an easier time managing them.

Derek's inability to pick up on expectations and feedback causes him to overstep both school and personal boundaries. His teachers will help him learn to use self-monitoring and corrective feedback to learn from his mistakes rather than keep repeating them. He also needs to become aware of what triggers his fits of anger.

Interventions That Help with Impulse Control and Self-Monitoring

I'm presenting these interventions in the context of Miss Kenny's social studies and Mr. Zornes's science classrooms, but these strategies can be easily adjusted to fit any grade level or content area. If, like these teachers, you have in your class several students who have delayed development of impulse control, there probably will be little learning for anyone until the students develop some control and

6.1 | Root Causes of Impulsiveness and Poor Self-Monitoring

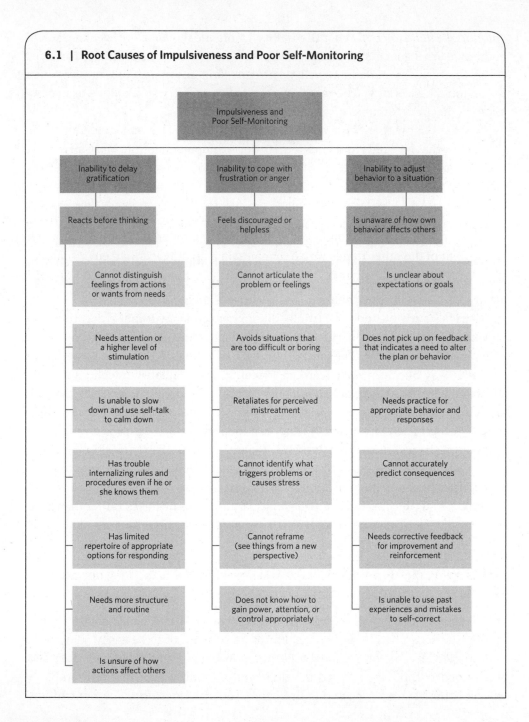

self-monitoring skills. Applying the interventions to the whole group over consecutive classes is the most effective way to build skills and ensure a cooperative classroom. However, you can use these strategies with any number of students—from the whole group to small groups to individuals (as we'll see later in this chapter's problem-solving case study)—and you do not need to use all the interventions or use them in sequence to see students make gains. Just make sure you are carefully choosing the techniques that best fit your students' root causes. The most important part of implementing these interventions is for you to believe that kids will do what it takes to be successful if they possibly can. It does take a significant amount of time and patience to teach students self-management skills and ways to cope with frustration, but it makes more of a difference in their lives than 90 percent of the other things we do to maintain a healthy learning environment.

In the following scenario, Miss Kenny and Mr. Zornes work together with the reinforcement of the counselor, Mrs. Hetrich, to help students develop better impulse control by understanding why people make the choices they do. Like most teachers, Miss Kenny and Mr. Zornes begin every school year by teaching skills like observing, recording, asking relevant questions, and considering options. This year, the two teachers are starting off with an interdisciplinary unit on how brain functioning and experiences affect our emotions and every decision we make. The investigating skills coincide with Common Core standards in both content areas and will do double duty for students like Scott, Melissa, and Derek to help them develop the impulse control and collaboration skills needed for a smoothly operating classroom.

Building Language for Managing Emotions

Sometimes out-of-control behavior is a mental processing problem rather than an attitude issue. When students gain a better understanding of how their brains work, they have an easier time taking charge of them. They need to know that strong and negative emotions (feeling left out, resentful, frustrated, and so on) are common to everyone. They also need to understand that although people cannot control how they feel, tempering reactions to these emotions is what happy, successful people have learned to do. Many students' inability to manage their emotions stems from their limited capacity to express themselves clearly.

VOCABULARY CONTINUUM STRATEGY. For this strategy, students create a chart that ranks families of adjectives in order from a negative to a positive extreme. For example: *miserable*, *awful*, *poor*, *average*, *good*, *excellent*, and *superb*.

Students like Derek and Melissa will be more likely to solve problems by talking them through rather than acting out if they have the words to describe what is going on with them emotionally. Mr. Zornes also knows that both of these students will need to work on using precise language when writing responses and lab reports. Both Miss Kenny and Mr. Zornes will use this vocabulary continuum strategy to establish common language in a variety of areas. For now, Mr. Zornes is concentrating on having students identify and label ranges of feelings. After modeling for the whole class how to arrange a few sets of continuum cards from negative to positive, he lists the following basic emotions on the board: *flexible, uncertain, thoughtful, calm,* and *satisfied*. He explains that the students will be working with partners to choose one of the feelings listed and think of their own range of emotions on both the positive and negative sides of the "starter" feeling. Before they work on their own, Mr. Zornes gives them an example:

> I'm going to choose the feeling *contented* as my starting emotion. On the positive side, a better feeling than *contented* is *happy,* and better than happy is *ecstatic*. On the negative side, less than contented is *unhappy*, and the most extreme negative feeling I can think of on that end of the range is *miserable*. Help me think of other feelings to add to this emotion chart.

Next, Mr. Zornes tells the partners to select an emotion from the board and work on their own continuums. They only need to add one or two emotion words to the spectrum before passing the chart to the next pair of students to add words. The exercise continues until each emotion continuum contains at least seven words. This activity gives students practice in the Common Core skills of describing and classifying and results in rich debate between partners. It also establishes a strong working vocabulary for the next step in learning to recognize emotions and becoming aware of the body signals related to these different feelings.

Reading Your Body Signals

Once the language to describe emotions is in place, students need to recognize the physical signals the human body sends when the emotional brain is initiating a hijack. Mr. Zornes uses a brainstorming activity to do that. He introduces the strategy by telling students its purpose:

> What floats your personal boat or sinks it? Let's find out, because you cannot stop your emotions from hijacking your brain unless you can feel the emotions coming. First, I want you to brainstorm a list of unconscious physical signals— not thoughts—that can occur when people go from feeling relaxed to angry.

Students list some typical signals: "I start breathing harder, my muscles tighten, my face gets red, my eyes narrow, my heart beats faster and I sweat, my stomach has a knot, my voice gets higher and louder, I pull away and clench my fists, my forehead scrunches up." Mr. Zornes is happy to see that Derek is taking part in this discussion, since he is the student most vulnerable to angry emotional outbursts. Mrs. Hetrich, the counselor, will follow up with Derek on practicing and applying the learning from this activity when his small group on anger management meets.

After they list physical signals for a few more positive and negative emotions, Mr. Zornes asks partners to choose an "emotion continuum" from the first exercise and identify physical signs they might use to figure out where they are on that range of emotions.

Some pairs of students decide to report out by including the physical signals on the continuum, some demonstrate using a charade game, and a few decide to write a report that explains their findings. No matter which reporting system they choose, students must cite at least one credible source that verifies their information. Because there are only six computers in his room, Mr. Zornes provides some partners with articles while others do their own search. One pair of students discovers the Plutchik Wheel of Emotions and suggests that the class make its own version of this wheel based on the information it collected about emotions. (Try a web search for this infograph. It's a great tool!)

With the language for describing emotions and identifying signals in place, Mr. Zornes moves to exploring "emotional triggers" (thoughts, feelings, or events that cause stress).

Identifying Emotional Triggers

Every day we experience demanding or stressful situations. Some events or people hold an emotional charge for us and trigger intense reactions such as frustration, insecurity, anger, resentment, jealousy, or defensiveness. If left unmanaged, negative emotional triggers lead to stress and conflict. They drain us of mental energy and prevent us from having the types of relationships and success we really want. Mr. Zornes wants his students to develop an understanding of their personal triggers and how to manage them. He teaches them to listen to their body signals and catch themselves before they react in order to discover if the perceived threat is real or not.

Perceived emotional threats are actually about unmet needs like getting attention, being treated fairly, and feeling accepted, understood, in control, safe, competent, respected, needed, right, free, or included. Your brain is always on the lookout for anything that threatens these needs. The hard part is knowing whether the need is truly unmet or the threat is unfounded. In Melissa's case, she feels that her need for being in control is threatened when teachers tell her what to do. At home, her entire world feels out of control because of ongoing family problems, so at school she seeks ways to regain some power. The problem is she doesn't know how to get power in productive ways, and she doesn't realize that the teachers are not the real threat to her sense of control. If she cannot put her finger on the specific need that is triggering her negative reactions, she will be in the dark as to what the real problem is and continue to beat her head against an unforgiving wall.

Mr. Zornes uses another continuum strategy to teach students about triggers and how to develop a hypothesis after making observations. This time, the continuum is marked on the floor by a line of tape. The left side of the line represents "an extremely negative emotional response," while the right side represents "an extremely positive feeling." Mr. Zornes begins by having eight students stand on the line, then provides a prompt designed to elicit an emotional response. Each student then chooses the position on the line that best represents how the prompt makes him or her feel. When the prompt "riding a bike" is given, most students stand near the middle of the line, although a few stand farther to one side or the other. "Bungee jumping," however, scatters students to the extreme ends. Even though the groups of students and the prompts change, the pattern remains the same: students choose to stand in different places. As Mr. Zornes asks students to explain their choices, each has a story that makes his or her individual preference seem reasonable.

While some students are on the line, their classmates are recording their observations. Mr. Zornes asks students to pair up to discuss their observations from the exercise and develop a hypothesis about what makes people respond in different ways to the same prompt. The class's main conclusion is that the same event can trigger reactions ranging from extreme excitement to paralyzing fear depending on people's experiences or the mental images they hold onto. Mr. Zornes initiates a discussion by asking whether knowing that the same trigger can affect classmates in different ways will make it easier or harder to work in teams and with partners. He also asks, "How will this knowledge help you when you experience negative feelings about another person's idea or request?"

From the discussion, Mr. Zornes knows that his students are beginning to see that people make different choices based on their prior experiences and beliefs. Students are also building the skills of observation and drawing conclusions from data while they continue to become more conscious of how emotions work and why people react to the same stimulus in different ways. They are becoming conscious observers of their own emotional experiences, as well. Miss Kenny will take this discussion to higher levels by having students use their new insights to analyze how the experiences and beliefs of leaders and citizens throughout history influenced their decisions. Mrs. Hetrich also follows up by applying this learning to her private counseling sessions with Melissa on how to gain power without trying to snatch it from the people who are trying to help her. Now students can begin the more difficult steps of learning to manage emotions.

Anchoring

Certain triggers—images, people, tastes, smells, and sounds—elicit strong emotions, and these can anchor to another idea or emotion. *Anchoring* is a process that happens when a stimulus wires itself to a subconscious or automatic response. For example, when Derek sits next to Jeremy, teachers know an argument is soon to follow because they constantly set each other off, and when Melissa feels that a teacher puts her on the spot, her default response is to announce how "lame" this class is. Anchors can work for you or against you and are at play in many of our reactions and choices. Advertisers know this and work hard to anchor certain emotions and responses to their products.

Miss Kenny will use ads as a way of introducing this concept to her students as well as teaching the skills of observing and analyzing patterns. She starts by asking the class some opening questions: "What subconscious things cause you to make the choices you do? Why choose a Coke instead of a Pepsi? Why buy a name brand when the house brand is sometimes the exact same product? Why do you decide to act silly in one class and never consider it in another?"

Miss Kenny then shows students a video clip of a TV commercial and has them list all the strong emotions they think the ad agency is trying to arouse. She lists some major emotions, values, and urges to look for: fear, love, guilt, comfort, trust, value, belonging, competition, instant gratification, leadership, trendsetting, and desire for free time and fun.

The class analyzes the first commercial together, which depicts a happy family of fuzzy blue cartoon bears living in an upscale home. They decide that the commercial triggers feelings of caring for family; valuing money, warmth, comfort, and trendsetting (everybody's doing it); and guilt (good moms buy this product), to name a few. They discuss why the ad agency wants the viewer's brain to link, or anchor, these emotional triggers to their brand of toilet paper and examine how repeated viewing strengthens the link by practicing the association and leads to a subconscious choice of the product in the grocery store.

Next, Miss Kenny asks students to apply what they have learned about anchoring in the more neutral context of ads to more personal contexts:

> Can you think of ways anchoring happens to you in school? Is there a certain person who instantly makes you want to have fun by fooling around all the time, or a certain type of assignment that subconsciously makes you think you are not capable? What can you do to make sure these triggers don't hijack your brain?

The students are surprised to learn that the answer is the same as the problem: anchoring. Miss Kenny tells the students that as they study history, they will keep this idea of anchoring in mind, make hypotheses about why leaders and citizens made the choices they did, and discuss which choices the students would have made had they been in the historical figures' shoes. Miss Kenny then previews the next day's activity, telling students they will investigate ways to use anchoring with self-calming techniques to help regain control over their emotions.

Learning Self-Calming Techniques

Our emotional brain is much faster at reacting than is our thinking brain, which is why Scott, Derek, and Melissa have such a hard time thinking before reacting. If thinking conflicts with emotion, emotion always wins—unless you know how to override the emotional hijack. Let's take Melissa's case of test anxiety. Even though she knows the material, her insecurities kick in, and she worries that she won't be able to remember it. This worry becomes a self-fulfilling prophecy, since her brain is now in the process of being hijacked.

Because emotionally hijacked brains usually make poor decisions, calming yourself down before you take a test, make a decision, or engage in a problem-solving conversation is in your own interest. It is best to first stop and take a breath, literally. Research (Cleveland Clinic, 2013) shows that deep breathing slows the heart rate, brings more oxygen to the brain, and lowers blood pressure, and these changes, in turn, help clear your head. Miss Kenny teaches the following steps to her class for ramping down anxiety and stress responses through self-calming and anchoring, while Mr. Zornes reinforces these same steps in science:

1. *Remove yourself.* If you feel stressed, it's best to remove yourself from the "scene of the crime" (the person, place, or event) that has triggered the hijack. Find a comfortable place to sit. Now sit with your back straight, stretch, yawn, and clear your mind.

2. *Breathe.* Breathe in deeply through your nose for a count of four seconds, hold for seven seconds, and then softly breathe out through your mouth for a count of nine seconds. Picture not blowing out a candle, but just making the flame dance around a bit. Repeat this deep breathing 10 to 20 times, and each time picture yourself exhaling tension.

3. *Think calming thoughts.* As you breathe, you can also use anchoring to change your upsetting thoughts and feelings to more peaceful and helpful ones. Think of calming things like a relaxing piece of music, the feeling of sunshine on your back, or the smell of hot apple pie—whatever mental image relaxes you the most. You will need to practice this regularly to get your anchor to wire itself so strongly that it will be second nature for you to calm yourself when you need to.

4. *Relax your muscles.* Now slowly start relaxing your muscles, starting with your face and moving to your neck, shoulders, and back. Relax your middle body and then go to your hips, knees, and feet. Keep breathing deeply and going back to your soothing mental pictures.

5. *Practice.* If you practice this technique every day, it will be easier to get your body to cooperate when you are upset. Remember that repeating the link over and over sets the anchor.

This self-calming procedure helps Derek and Scott shift from feelings of stress and excitement to calm and focus, and it helps Melissa move from feelings of boredom and hopelessness to alertness and confidence. They just need to use different mental images. Mr. Zornes follows the calm-down technique by asking students to imagine situations in which they would need to be pumped up instead of calmed down:

> Visualize how you want to be and how that would feel, and create a mental anchor for it. See if you can think of one example of when you would need to calm down in class and another of when you would need to pump up. Write those two examples in your journal and describe what mental image would help you anchor your emotions.

The students are beginning to make headway in building both emotional literacy and the crucial science and social studies skills of describing and predicting. Scott's impulsiveness, Melissa's defiance, and Derek's temper are still hard to deal with, however, so Mr. Zornes asks the counselor, Mrs. Hetrich, to do more of this self-calming work with them. The entire class needs these techniques, but these three students need more practice than the others do.

The next challenge for Mr. Zornes is to help students understand that it is not how something makes you feel that makes you jump for joy or fall apart; it is how you react to and handle those feelings. "How will you choose to react to whatever happens to you today?" will be Mr. Zornes's theme question as he addresses the internal triggers we create through stories we tell ourselves and how we can choose to change our story or reframe the situation. Over time, this reframing skill will enable students to take more responsibility for monitoring and adjusting their personal responses to emotions.

Reframing

Today Mr. Zornes works with his students on considering alternative explanations for things that happen. This is not only a critical skill for science investigations but also an essential part of managing behavior choices.

Reframing is the process of changing your expectations or perspective in order to make sense of a situation and get emotional relief. This process can turn around an emotional hijack and put you back in control of how your brain handles an emotional trigger. Sometimes our brain links a person, an activity, or a place to negative emotions. For example, if my friend comes up and slaps me on the back, I turn and smile because my brain says, "He likes me and wants me to know he is there." If a person I don't like slaps me on the back in the exact same way, I am not going to be happy because my brain says, "This jerk is messing with me." It has nothing to do with the slap on the back, and I may be misreading the intention of the person doing the slapping. My reaction is controlled by the mental story I tell myself. If I change my story to "maybe this guy wants to apologize," I change how I feel and I will most likely respond differently. Reframing changes the way you think and act by adding new information or a different perspective to your original thinking.

Negative emotional triggers often say more about how we feel about ourselves and our wounded pride than they do about the problem. Unless students can figure out what is really setting them off, they will never control their emotional triggers. Mr. Zornes gives some examples of hijacks in progress and asks his students for possible ways to mentally reframe the situations and relieve the stress:

> Every time Georgia sees Linda, she remembers the time Linda made her feel like an outcast. Now, just the sight of Linda or her sister makes Georgia bristle and want to make a catty, backstabbing comment about her. What story is Georgia telling herself that gives Linda the power to make her so uncomfortable? How can Georgia reframe this story to put herself back in control and soothe her jangled nerves? Instead of thinking, "She is snubbing me and trying to keep me from being included," Georgia could reframe it by thinking, "Linda may be shy and waiting for me to talk to her first" or "What if Linda needs attention and is afraid I will take the group's attention away from her?" Georgia's response will be quite different depending on what she chooses to believe about the situation.

> New problem, and this time it isn't a person. Let's say the prospect of giving an oral report is the emotional trigger that makes you feel like shutting down and clamming up. What story are you probably telling yourself that causes you to feel like a victim in this science class? It could be that you expect to fail because that has been your experience. We know everybody has a need to feel like a winner, and your self-talk says, "This is hopeless. I can't do it." What new story can you tell yourself that will relieve this stress? Good, realizing that you don't have to be perfect can help. Yes, admitting that you are intelligent but need to learn to study more would be useful. Right, telling yourself that you could do the work if you had some extra assistance is also a useful story. Now the new problem might be that you don't know how to get that help. What story would you need to tell yourself to get you over your reluctance to ask for what you need?

Mr. Zornes is happy with the progress he sees in his students' ability to be good observers and analyzers, especially in Melissa's case. He can see her attitude becoming more open and accepting. These are basic skills he will draw on all year long in every unit of science. He needs to teach one more skill for students to have the tools they need to take responsibility for their own emotional and academic learning.

Self-Monitoring

As we have seen, the executive skill of self-monitoring has a role in every other category of executive function, and for impulse control, it is supremely important. Evaluating their own decisions builds students' self-confidence by helping them see that they have control over their choices. They begin to understand that they can get more of what they want by changing the way they act. Learning self-monitoring skills is one more step toward being in control of their own behavior.

CHARTING FOR PATTERNS. People can predict what will cause success by looking for patterns of good results and patterns that cause errors. To spot these patterns, top athletes, musicians, and performers analyze video recordings of their performances. When they see what went right, they repeat it. When they spot what went wrong, they work on improving specific skills to get better results. When we don't see patterns, we just do what we usually do, and this means making the same errors over and over.

Mr. Zornes explains this common practice of successful people to his students. He wants them to know that making a mistake once or twice is normal, but making the same mistake repeatedly signals a problem that needs to be solved. If they don't address this problem, they will likely become overly frustrated and argue or do something else that results in a loss of privileges. He sets up a class self-monitoring task, telling students that it will help them learn to recognize clues and patterns in what is going wrong and to analyze how well they are using what they've learned about taking control of their emotional life and time.

At first, he sets a timer to go off every 10 minutes; later, it will go off at random times. When the timer dings, students record on a chart what they are doing. For example, they might be reading, listening to a lecture, working on a lab report, or staring off into space. Next, they jot down how well their choice worked and how they felt about it. One person may feel frustrated while working on his lab, while another is excited or happy. Students also list a couple of choices (either better or poorer) they could have made at the time but didn't. Finally, they note what they might choose to do next time that would have better results. Some parts of

6.2 | Sample Self-Monitoring Chart for Improving Choices

Time	What I was doing	How did it turn out?	Other choices I had	What I will do next time
9:00	Listening to lecture	Pretty well	Daydreaming or taking better notes	Use split-page notes—they are easier to read.
9:10	Working with Frank	OK, but I'm a little frustrated.	Doing less talking about last night or moving to another desk	Change the subject so we get more work done.
9:20	Working with the group but I shut down	It stunk—I felt angry.	Speaking up more or complaining about how they ignore my ideas	I'm not sure what I will actually do about this.

the journal can be filled in at the end of class, but students need to make sure they capture what they are doing every 10 minutes. Mr. Zornes shares an example of a student's chart (see Figure 6.2) from the year before with his class.

This intervention is particularly helpful for Scott, who can now see that he is off task quite a bit more than he is on task. This awareness helps him use the next intervention of internal coaching more efficiently.

JOURNALING TO DEVELOP AN INTERNAL COACH. Participating in learning activities or experiences doesn't result in learning; it's reflecting on those activities that teaches us. Sometimes we need to retrain ourselves to think about things differently. This is called developing an *internal coach*. Your internal coach has the ability to reframe a sticky situation or verbalize self-instructions, such as when Derek spaces out and needs to say to himself, "Wait, I skipped part of that problem" or "That passage doesn't make sense to me, so here is what I can do. . . ." Sometimes Melissa's internal coach needs to give her a pep talk so she doesn't wallow in self-pity, blame, or negative thinking ("I'm not smart enough" or "My whole day is ruined, and I'm too stressed and tired for this"). Scott's internal coach needs to say things like "Wait a minute. Is this a good idea? What are my other choices?"

To develop an effective internal coach, students need guided practice in self-monitoring. They need to reflect on how useful their responses and choices are for both themselves and others, especially in collaborative classrooms.

At the end of each day at Mr. Zornes's school, all the 7th grade teachers have students write a three-minute post in their emotional literacy journals. After looking at the patterns in their charts for the day, the students act as their own internal coaches by asking themselves questions like

- Was I productive today? If not, what am I saying to myself when I go off task? Am I giving up?
- Did what I was reading or hearing make sense to me? Did I need to ask a question?
- Am I confident that I can be successful?
- How did I handle things that distracted or upset me? Should I have reframed a situation to reduce my stress? (Meichenbaum & Goodman, 1971)

The teachers check a few student journals each day and have a two-minute conference with each of those students on the decisions they are making and how these decisions are affecting their day. Teaching self-reflection not only fosters more responsible decision making but also helps teachers manage student-centered classrooms. The teachers know that the more self-monitoring is practiced, the more automatic it becomes, so they include some type of self-monitoring in every class. As students learn to define problems, ask relevant questions, and evaluate options, they develop a life skill that will serve them well in every phase of their lives.

Practicing Collaboration Skills

If we cannot learn to manage strong emotions, there are going to be social consequences. Miss Kenny wants her classroom to be a safe and welcoming environment for learning. She uses the new emotional awareness her students have been developing to teach cooperation and leadership, skills that are essential to the environment she wants to create. Communication is critical to collaborative relationships, so she starts there.

READING NONVERBALS. Researchers estimate that we express 90 percent or more of our communications nonverbally, so obviously, being able to interpret nonverbal communication is a foundation for building good relationships (Tannen, 1998). Children and adolescents process body language in the part of the brain that handles emotion, whereas adults process nonverbals in the analytical part of the brain. No wonder our three students are so likely to misinterpret body language and misunderstand friends and adults. They are frequently missing the nuances of nonverbal cues.

Miss Kenny teaches her students how to read nonverbal signals (facial expressions, gestures, eye contact, posture, and tone of voice) so they can respond more purposefully. This will be an important lesson for Derek and Scott, since they are often oblivious to how their actions are affecting other people. Miss Kenny uses first a game and then a collage activity to help students relate to the concept. She introduces her version of charades to her class:

> When I say "Now," I want you to strike a body pose that tells me how you feel about snakes without making a sound. "Now." First row, freeze in that position, and the rest of us are going to analyze your messages. Yes, we get the picture that Carl isn't afraid. How could you tell? Right, eyebrows up, mouth in a relaxed smile, hands holding the snake, body forward as if he is interested. Now look at Patty: squinty eyes, body pulled back, hand over her mouth like she might throw up, shoulders forward, hands clenched, and so is her jaw. She looks repulsed by the snake rather than afraid of it. As we look at our classmates, we can see how they convey their feelings without telling us anything with words. We have to be careful, though, because we can misinterpret these signals. Some cultures attach different meanings to body language, but most are similar.

The class members continue to take turns freezing in their body language responses to Miss Kenny's prompts and analyzing the nonverbals they see. When Miss Kenny is satisfied that they have the hang of looking for nonverbal cues, she asks each student to pull from a box a piece of paper on which she has written an emotion. Their assignment is to create a scrapbook of drawn or cut-out pictures (from magazines, ads, etc.) of body language and to describe how these body signals represent the chosen emotion.

Goleman says that being able to tune into another person's feelings and understand how they think is essential to being a great collaborator, team player, and negotiator. Becoming adept at interpreting body language takes time, effort, and perseverance. Practice will help us get better at becoming aware of physical signals, but we also need to practice improving the way we listen to people.

ACTIVE LISTENING. Listening with empathy is crucial to collaboration. We need practice to become aware of and limit our personal filters as we listen to others. Paraphrasing and reflective listening are two powerful strategies that help us accomplish this. Mr. Zornes teaches both skills with an active listening exercise.

He pays special attention to Scott and Derek, who have particular trouble internalizing what they hear.

Mr. Zornes starts the demonstration by asking Derek and Jacob to pretend they are having a problem with being lab partners: they both want the job of group leader. In this exercise, each partner must try to convince the other that he should be the leader. Mr. Zornes instructs them to hold their ground as they make their cases in front of the class. When he thinks they have argued long enough, he stops the conversations and starts the debrief:

> Derek and Jacob, how did that conversation make you feel? Were you listening to your partner? What did you think he was saying, Derek? Is that what you meant, Jacob? That was frustrating for both of you, wasn't it? OK, now we are going to change this activity. You will have the same conversation, but this time, each of you will take a turn paraphrasing what the other person said and reflecting on what you heard before you make your next point. I will help you if you get stuck along the way.
>
> Jacob, I want you to listen carefully as Derek makes his point and then restate in your own words exactly what you think he was trying to say to you. Make sure you make eye contact and observe his body language as well as listen to his words. Try not to think of arguments or your point of view as you listen. Remember, you don't have to agree or disagree with what he said, just restate his feeling and thoughts accurately.

Jacob listens and paraphrases what he heard: "Derek feels frustrated because he hasn't been the group leader for a long time. He feels like we don't think he is capable." Mr. Zornes checks with Derek, who says Jacob got it right. Then Derek takes a turn actively listening and reflecting as Jacob explains how he feels. After Derek paraphrases Jacob accurately, Mr. Zornes sums up the activity:

> Great job. Is it going to be easier for you to figure out how to solve the problem now that you have listened to each other? One thing that helps is putting aside your personal agenda long enough to communicate. Knowing that you are both going to be heard before the decision is made also makes it easier to listen to each other.

Zig Ziglar famously said, "You can get everything in life you want if you will just help enough other people get what they want." Learning and practicing collaboration and problem-solving skills go a long way toward creating productive relationships and high-performing classrooms. The 7th grade teachers with their three impulsive students are on the way to enjoying collaborative student-centered classrooms.

Establishing Routines and Accountability

As a result of teaching emotional awareness and coping skills, the 7th grade teachers' discussions now have less to do with investing in Ritalin dart guns for controlling behavior and more to do with developing ways to increase the type of student engagement that promotes independence and student responsibility.

Research (Lambert & McCombs, 1998) shows that successful students are actively involved in their own learning, monitor their thinking, think about their learning, and assume responsibility for their learning. The team knows this research and is now able to shift to a student-centered instructional approach. The teachers allocate at least 50 percent of each period as student processing time, during which students actively engage in applying skills and synthesizing knowledge for problem solving. During this time, cooperative learning, conferencing with students, and small-group instruction come into play.

While teachers are giving small-group instruction, other students have time to work on assignments at various stations. When routines and procedures are carefully taught and consistently reinforced, students actually stay on task for the most part. The stations hold challenging and engaging assignments that take the place of boring, one-size-fits-all worksheets and end-of-chapter assignments. These tasks reinforce and extend what students learned in class. Each station is set up in tiers of color-coded activities. Yellow-coded assignments are entry-level tasks that students may use if they need prerequisite and practice skills before taking on more challenging work. Green-coded assignments are application-level assignments requiring students to solve two-step problems that apply skills in combination. Blue-coded tasks are the most challenging problems and may require more than one class period to complete. Mr. Zornes and Miss Kenny give guidelines based on assessment results that help students figure out which stations they need to do first and which level to start with. Not all students are expected to complete all levels of all stations, but there are enough options available that there is never downtime. Before students were taught to monitor and control their own behavior, this would have been a risky plan. Now it works like a charm most days, although there are still students who require close monitoring and numerous reminders.

The teachers have incorporated clear, reasonable limits and expectations into the daily routines, but not too many. Besides how to set up and clean up, there are consistent guidelines about what to do at each station, how long to stay, exactly how to work with a partner, and how to solve problems individually. These opportunities are essential to developing good independent work skills. The more loosey-goosey the routines, the greater the possibility of poor results.

If students violate the procedures, the teacher stops them and asks what guideline they are forgetting. The teachers find that using humor to make the point is generally the most effective intervention, but they never confuse humor with sarcasm. If a student has to be removed from a station activity, there is always a reentry strategy that helps the student feel welcomed back and redirected.

Structure is essential for building student confidence and independence, but without a consistent accountability system in place, the entire system can fall apart. Students receive points for learning from their station activities, not just for doing the activities. Both oral and written mini-quizzes are scheduled regularly upon completion of a station. Teachers try to check the learning of six or seven students each day by having two-minute conferences with them. This informs the students of what needs to be redone and keeps them honest when it comes to thinking through the work.

Self-assessment is just as important as teacher feedback. Students need to analyze how this cooperative and independent learning is working for them and give evidence that supports their claim. Keeping charts of their learning gains helps students draw more accurate conclusions and create plans for making the system better. By verbalizing options for improvement, students are able to see that they control their own choices and outcomes, which leads to better decision making.

Five-Step Problem-Solving Case Study: Impulsiveness and Weak Self-Monitoring

We're going to leave Miss Kenny and Mr. Zornes's classes to concentrate on an 8-year-old who is having problems with impulse control. Unlike Scott, Melissa, and Derek, he is not disruptive to the whole class. In fact, he often removes himself from the room when he loses control. Flight is Ronald's go-to behavior when his thinking brain is hijacked by emotion:

Ronald has dreams of being an A student but believes that can never happen. Every time he has to speak in class or take a test, his heart pounds wildly, his stomach knots up, and his palms break out in a sweat. His gut tells him to shoot out the door and keep on running, and he has been known to do just that. Ronald feels helpless when the work is challenging, so he generally gives up or puts down any answer that seems close. He doesn't want to ask for help out of fear of looking stupid in front of his friends, so he just suffers in silence and expects to fail.

Mrs. Fulton, Ronald's teacher, has tried to talk to him about his anxiety, but her efforts only upset him more. The school has a supportive and collaborative staff, so Mrs. Fulton feels comfortable turning to colleagues for ideas.

Step 1. Know the Student

Mrs. Fulton and Mr. Sheets, the special education teacher and school's problem-solving coach, put their heads together about Ronald. They identify concerns both for behavior and academics and a long list of strengths (see Figure 6.3). Mrs. Fulton

---

6.3 | Strengths and Concerns Chart for Ronald

Name: Ronald Corwin
Grade: 3

Academic concerns:	Behavior concerns:
• Poor at math computation • Weak problem-solving skills in all classes • Comprehension is slightly below average • Writes minimal answers	• Seldom raises hand in class • Gives up when work gets hard • Cries or runs away when he is frustrated • Complains of being sick when work is hard
Strengths to build on:	
• Good word attack skills • Speaking and reading vocabularies are strong • Pleasant attitude when not frustrated • Reads 90 words correct per minute	• Loves all sports and plays soccer and baseball • Has three very good friends • Parents are very involved • Loves his little sister

knows Ronald has a lot going for him if only she can find some solutions for his frustration, fear, and flight pattern.

Step 2. Analyze the Root Causes

The coach keeps the flowchart of root causes of impulsiveness and poor self-monitoring (Figure 6.1) in front of him as he kicks off the discussion with Mrs. Fulton. He begins the analysis with "why" questions.

Coach: Why do you think Ronald gives up so easily?

Mrs. Fulton: He just doesn't seem to have any self-confidence.

Coach: What causes his confidence to be so low?

Mrs. Fulton: That's a mystery, because he typically has the skill to do what I assign. The minute things get hard, he panics and shuts down, and once he does that, the ball game is over for him.

Coach: So his fear of failure triggers his anxiety, and once he panics he cannot calm himself down? Or is he trying to exert his power?

Mrs. Fulton: It's not about power. He is a cooperative student who desperately wants to do well. He just cannot handle frustration. Once he gets upset, his distress escalates if anyone tries to talk to him, and he is likely to bolt out the door.

Coach: So what is he doing or thinking that causes this escalation?

Mrs. Fulton: I wish I knew.

Coach: Looking at this chart [Figure 6.1], let me suggest a couple of possibilities that might fit Ronald. He seems to avoid difficult situations and automatically expects to fail, so he shuts down. He may see shutting down and bolting as his only choices for coping: that's his default, so that's what he does. He also may not know how to calm himself down enough to think of other options for coping.

Mrs. Fulton: Yes, and he is hypersensitive to the possibility of doing things wrong.

Coach: OK, see if this sounds right. He needs to learn to calm himself down and learn to generate alternative choices that help him see that he can cope with his frustration in new ways.

Mrs. Fulton: That sounds like a good place to start. We also need to build his confidence by starting with activities that give him high success levels and slowly build in challenges. I know that works for him.

Step 3. Set a Clear and Measurable Goal

Mrs. Fulton and the coach agree on the root causes of Ronald's problems, and together they formulate a hypothesis and measurable outcomes to work toward.

Hypothesis: If we can teach Ronald strategies for calming himself and thinking through options and their consequences, he will make better choices for coping with his frustrations.

Time frame and measurement benchmarks: As a result of six weeks of training, Ronald will be able to calm himself down and choose a good solution at least once a day. His incidences of shutting down will go from an average of four times a day to no more than twice a day, and he will not leave school without permission.

Step 4. Decide How to Monitor Growth

Ronald stays with Mrs. Fulton all day except for his tutoring session with Mr. Blakley, the math tutor. After modeling and teaching numerous strategies, either Mrs. Fulton or Mr. Blakley will help Ronald choose one tough problem he faced each day and fill out a chart describing how he handled it. Figure 6.4 shows one of Ronald's completed charts.

6.4 | Ronald's Self-Monitoring Chart for Problem Solving

Problem:	How well did your solution work?	Monday's response	Tuesday's response	Wednesday's response	Thursday's response	Friday's response
Math paper	OK	Asked for help				
Writing assignment	Bad		Stopped working			
Writing assignment	Pretty good			Asked for a partner to get me started and used my calm down trick		

The teachers have a short discussion with Ronald asking what options he considered before making his choice. Ronald takes the charts to his Tuesday and Thursday sessions with the school counselor. Three other students join Ronald's session after three weeks, which helps him see that he is not the only student who finds it hard to face his fears and figure out new choices.

Step 5. Select an Action Plan from a List of Options

Ronald's team selects interventions that they think match the root causes of his problems, and they put together an action plan (see Figure 6.5) that lists strategies for teachers, for Ronald, and for his parents to use to build skills.

ROLE-PLAY SCENARIOS. The counselor describes a series of uncomfortable situations and asks Ronald to choose one word from a selection that matches how

6.5 | Action Plan for Ronald

Skills Needed	Teaching Strategies	Student Responsibilities	Suggestions for Parents
Self-calming	Begin guiding deep breathing and visualization.	Explain when you will use this and practice self-calming for two minutes a day as homework.	Practice calming strategy with Ronald daily.
Awareness of emotional hijack feelings	Counselor will role-play to model good awareness and problem-solving scenarios with Ronald.	Teach parents how to tell if you are getting upset and discuss how you want them to help you.	Remind Ronald to watch his body signals when you see that he is getting upset.
Awareness of options and consequences	Counselor will play "what would be another way" game. Teacher will use this game in science and social studies class.	Fill in the options you chose on your reporting sheet.	Ask Ronald what options he is thinking about when you ask him to do chores. Accept good and poor options and then ask which will work better.
Acceptance of feedback	Start giving feedback on papers in small doses. First ask Ronald for "one good thing and one thing to improve" on his paper. Then add another good thing and one thing to improve.	Think of "one good thing and one thing to improve" for at least one paper each day.	Model how you give yourself feedback using the "one good thing and one thing to improve" model on your work around the house, and ask Ronald to do the same for his work.

this scenario would make him feel. For example, the situation might be working on a science investigation that isn't going well, and the counselor offers an assortment of five cards reading "happy," "OK," "sad," "frustrated," and "angry." Ronald must pick a card and then describe how his body would let him know how upset he is. He rates his level of upset on a scale of 1 to 5 and discusses ways he could calm himself down to prevent a problem from occurring. The counselor then models different ways she might calm herself down and asks Ronald to try a couple of these methods before selecting what works best for him.

"WHAT WOULD BE ANOTHER WAY" GAME. This game starts by introducing a series of problem situations in which a student makes a less-than-ideal choice, like pushing in line or not asking for help when confused. The student playing the game describes one or two possible consequences of this choice, rates it on a scale ranging from 1 (an OK choice) to 5 (a very bad choice), and explains why he or she rated it that way. Students use four criteria to guide their rating:

1. Does the choice do more harm than good?
2. Does it consider other people's feelings and needs?
3. How well does it follow the rules for safety?
4. Does it help me learn?

A sample problem might be, "Judy asks Donna to hold the paper while she cuts out the pieces they need for the poster. Donna is reluctant to do this but decides to comply rather than make her friend angry. What are the possible consequences of this choice? What rating would you give it? What would be another way to handle this situation?"

"ONE GOOD THING AND ONE THING TO IMPROVE." Ronald has a hard time accepting the fact that everyone makes mistakes and needs to learn from them rather than try to hide them or avoid difficult tasks. This activity is an easy way to help young students start using criteria to judge their own performance. Children can be overwhelmed by too much feedback, so the activity should start with pointing out just one good thing and making one suggestion for improvement. For example, Ellen saw that her friend Connie was struggling with her math work and offered to help. Ellen then wrote down the answers to all the problems Connie was unable to complete. What one good thing did Ellen do? What suggestion do you have for making Ellen's effort to help better? Mrs. Fulton will do a few similar activities with the whole class, which will show Ronald how to relieve stress by learning to address problems in a positive way.

Large-Group Application

Mrs. Fulton knows that all the students in her class have to cope with a certain degree of anxiety and frustration as they face academic and emotional challenges. The students who are able to slow down and think before they act will have an easier time rising to such occasions than will those who are more impulsive because of an executive dysfunction. Mrs. Fulton has several effective strategies that will provide structure and support for the more impulsive students while teaching even the most mature children valuable life strategies for learning from mistakes and internalizing routines and procedures using positive thinking and problem solving.

THE GEEK SQUAD BOARD. Students like Ronald have little faith in their ability to succeed. They think, "If it's hard for me, then I must be dumb." Mrs. Fulton wants her students to instead think, "If it's hard, then I will have to stretch myself, and sometimes that means I need to ask for help." She often asks students, "What made you get better at that?" to encourage them to see themselves as good problem solvers. She goes the extra mile by providing a bulletin board she calls the *Geek Squad board* (inspired by the tech support company) that is a dedicated space for students to post their imperfect work, accompanied by notes describing how they fixed their own problems. This gives kids bragging rights for learning from their mistakes and helps other students see new options when they experience the same types of difficulty. Students who used to see problems as sources of stress and embarrassment soon learn that there is another way to view these situations.

AUTHOR'S CHAIR. Ronald is not the only student in the class who needs help accepting feedback and using it to improve. A hallmark of a safe and disciplined learning environment is students who help one another improve by graciously giving and receiving useful feedback. Mrs. Fulton teaches her students to use the *author's chair* to support and improve work rather than simply judge it. Students learn that grades, scores, and statements like "That was good" or "I didn't like that" do not qualify as helpful. Helpful feedback indicates specifically what is worth keeping and what needs to change.

Mrs. Fulton starts by sitting in the author's chair herself, with six class members (the review committee) sitting at her feet. The rest of the class observes as she models the process. First, Mrs. Fulton reads an anchor paper (a paper from last year's class) and asks her reviewers to list two good things about the writing. The review committee reaches a consensus and then selects the very best thing about this paper. Mrs. Fulton then has the group brainstorm two ideas for improving the paper. Again, the committee selects the most helpful piece of advice to give to the author. This process demonstrates how to give precise feedback on what to keep and what to change to make a piece of writing more interesting to a reader. Mrs. Fulton models this strategy for several days before asking students to plan their own feedback sessions for a pretend classmate. Later they will use this same process to review and make suggestions for one another's actual work.

CLASS MEETINGS. The same idea behind the author's chair strategy can be used to improve the classroom environment and help students internalize the reasons for rules and procedures. Students are invited to drop suggestions into the "Ideas for Improvement" jar any time they have a specific idea or complaint that they would like the class to address. For example, Mrs. Fulton put in a complaint that students were wasting learning time by being too rowdy as they came in from recess. Jeremy anonymously complained that he was feeling left out because no one wanted to be his partner on Tuesday. The class took a few minutes to list ways to solve both of these problems and agreed to decide on a fix-up plan for the problems at the next class meeting.

Mrs. Fulton sees that class meetings focus on solving problems without blaming anyone. This positive approach to problem solving is shifting the class's climate from cliquish and competitive to caring and cooperative. The safe environment is also helping Ronald shift from being a frequent "runner" in times of frustration to being a student who feels confident enough to rise to the challenges that school presents.

Summary

When we are stressed, chemicals in our brains shut off our resourcefulness—a phenomenon commonly referred to as *emotional hijacking*. When students understand how emotional hijacking happens, they have a better chance of applying strategies that help prevent or reverse the takeover. Teachers who intentionally teach skills like self-calming, reframing, and self-monitoring make it possible for students to harness impulsiveness.

Teaching self-monitoring skills enables students to repeat things that work and avoid behaviors that prevent them from meeting their goals. Students who are less likely to learn from their mistakes because of executive functioning delays need small-group modeling with lots of guided practice as well as classroom practice with peers. This skill will be especially helpful as they collaborate with other people and take on more responsibility for themselves.

WHAT WORKS: Slowing down students' thinking; replaying experiences and analyzing why students reacted the way they did; using skits and film clips to practice interpreting body language; considering possible solutions and consequences; practicing active listening to keep students from becoming defensive; teaching students to adjust their choices and behaviors to fit the circumstances; using checklists, rubrics, and self-questioning to reflect on actions; providing direct feedback and having students check that feedback with their perceptions; listening to students' versions and interpretations of events and letting them compare theirs with yours; teaching self-talk to help students develop an internal coach.

WHAT DOESN'T WORK: Yelling, lecturing, or showing frustration or anxiety; removing "problem" students from the group; assuming students can control their impulsivity; attending to each disruption; humiliating students; arguing or challenging students' excuses; assuming students are repeating poor behaviors out of meanness or obstinacy.

How well students learn to self-monitor and manage their emotions has a lot to do with the emotional tone the teacher sets. A safe, accepting, and welcoming classroom environment makes it easier for students to control their behavior, develop a sense of independence, and accept responsibility. In classrooms where the teacher believes in the students, differentiates the work, and sets up consistent supportive routines and procedures, students have a better chance of maturing both emotionally and academically.

On Your Own

Try using the five-step problem-solving process to help one of our case study students.

Case study 1. *Phillip is only in 4th grade, and he is already the poster child for the inability to anticipate consequences. He doesn't have his report and is furious with his mother for not putting it in his book bag. It never occurs to him that the problem might have been caused by his flying out of the house without checking. This seems to happen at least once a week, and yet his plan, or lack of one, doesn't change. Phillip scans rather than reads the assigned science chapter and is totally surprised to receive another 65 percent on the test. The soccer coach benches him for not having his jersey; of course, the custodian who* *would not let him back into school after hours is to blame. Phillip constantly vacillates between dawdling and rushing, without taking responsibility for the bad results.*

Case study 2. *Magdalena is a beautiful 15-year-old who has lots of friends but is as flighty as they come and a major drama queen. Although she has a solid IQ score, she does not strike any of her teachers as the brightest beacon in the harbor. It is hard for her to pay attention in class, and she sits there like a bump on a log, but the minute she gets into the hallway she erupts like a well-shaken can of pop. She alternates between shrieking like she's being executed when she sees a friend to sobbing because of a crude comment someone reported overhearing in the restroom. If a teacher asks her to simmer down, her immediate response is to blame someone else before going home and regaling her parents with stories about how all the teachers hate her. She doesn't see the patterns of how certain situations and friends tend to bring out the worst in her.*

CONCLUSION: TIPS FOR SUPPORTING STUDENTS

If Fran's memory and organization don't improve soon, all her missing and incomplete papers will result in one big, ugly report card. Fran has worked with Miss Williams to create a visual organization plan in the form of a checklist that she keeps taped to her desk. The list covers what Fran forgets most often: putting her name and date on the paper, labeling her answers, completing all the questions, and putting papers in the correct folder. Fran uses a colored pencil to put a check beside each item on her list as she completes it. She receives extra points for completing this checklist as part of her assignment. This plan will remain in place until checking becomes a habit for Fran; then Miss Williams will fade the intervention by taking one item off the checklist at a time to see if the job still gets done without the visual reminder.

Nolan's first impulse is to call people names when they upset him. "You stupid jerk" comes flying out of his mouth before he thinks. Mrs. Kilmer is tempted to say things like "Nolan, you are being rude to Ricardo again, and you're never going to have friends if you don't stop calling people names." She realizes, however, that labeling and judgmental talk sound like a lecture and don't teach Nolan to self-monitor, so she tries to use questions that state the problem objectively: "Nolan, I noticed you called Ricardo 'stupid' again today. Can you think of a kinder way to solve the problem?" Asking Nolan for alternative solutions is proving to be more helpful.

Marty gets in "the zone" when he is working. He does good work once he gets going, but it upsets him to switch to other tasks when he hasn't completed what he is working on. Mr. Marchetti knows that a heads-up a few minutes before it is time to stop working helps Marty make the transition from one activity to another more easily. Having enough time to shift his attention is an important intervention for Marty, who has refocusing and transition problems.

In this book, we have focused on students who have a hard time shifting mental gears, planning, remembering, processing information quickly, focusing attention, controlling impulses, and self-monitoring. These students struggle not because they won't ever be able to do these things, but because their executive thinking skills are still developing, so they find it difficult to manage without guidance. Threats and consequences stall these students rather than propel them, so, as shown in the examples above, teachers need to provide support if they want to see maximum growth.

Don't Label or Punish; *Do* Guide and Support

Concerns about poor planning and problem solving, weak memory, disorganization, inability to focus attention, impulsiveness, and poor self-monitoring can be a problem for students of any age. Typically, these issues become increasingly problematic around 4th grade, when expectations for independence go up just as the tight structure of early grades is lowered. In middle grades and high school, academic demands increase as adult support decreases, and students with weak executive skills experience growing frustration, even when their academic ability is solid.

Parents and teachers can reduce their own frustrations and those of the students by understanding that what appear to be laziness and lack of motivation are often an extreme need for support and guidance. Students with executive dysfunctions tend not to learn from previous experiences because they don't make cause-and-effect connections well, nor do they use feedback to adjust their plan of action. Saying things like "How many times have I told you not to do that?" or "We have been over and over this" or "I know you can do this because I've seen you do it before" only makes matters worse.

These students need targeted interventions. Designing these intervention plans requires careful diagnosis as well as knowledge of research-based strategies. Because some students require more of our time, energy, and guidance than others do, we must keep in mind that "fair" does not always mean "equal."

If we had the job of caring for a cactus, a violet, and a water lily, what would we do to ensure the growth of each? We would give each plant what it needs: more or less light, different types of soil, more or less water. With plants, it is obvious that a one-size-fits-all approach would be irresponsible. Sometimes it is harder to see that students have this same variety of needs. Assuming that the same level of support will work for all students is naive. It is also shortsighted to think that adults can make plans work effectively without buy-in from the student.

Develop a Plan *with* the Student, Not *for* the Student

Adults who plan *with* students instead of *for* them get a lot more cooperation. I am not talking about totally turning over the decision making to the student. What is needed is collaboration, involvement, and trust. These don't happen without a great system of communication and flexible thinking on the part of the adults. As a parent, I have sometimes found this thinking challenging to maintain but well worth the effort. Here's an example from my own experience.

My son needed to attend a problem-solving meeting at his high school. The night before, as we prepared for the meeting, each family member came up with possibilities for solving the problem of missing assignments. The next morning on the way to the meeting, my cranky son said, "I'm not going to talk at this meeting, and you can't make me." My emotional impulse was to stomp on his foot, but fortunately, my thinking brain took over, and I simply said instead,

> I know you are afraid the adults will gang up on you, but I promise you
> we won't let that happen. We are going to work out a mutually agreeable
> solution with you. You do understand that the assignments have to be done,
> right? There are lots of different ways to accomplish this. You are right that

I cannot make you talk if you decide not to, but if you help the team develop a plan, we can work together and make this problem go away. If you decide not to cooperate, your assignment problem will continue, and things will just get worse. We really want to help you be successful, but it is your choice.

Acknowledging his power helped my son decide not to use it as a weapon. If the adults in the meeting had not been respectful, I doubt the meeting would have had much effect. Showing respect by including students in the design of their plans is more likely to result in cooperation. I have applied this strategy at every grade level, preK–12, and have never regretted it. Collaboration helps students understand that it is good to be assertive and powerful, but with power comes responsibility. Sometimes when emotions remain high and adults exercise their power aggressively, the result is student retaliation, which helps no one.

It takes time and infinite patience to help some students get their act together. Modeling, corrective feedback, reassurance, and visual cuing are helpful in nurturing this process; harsh criticism generally sets students back.

So what does it take to make this problem-solving model a reality?

Checklist for Being a Guide

The saying "Be a guide on the side" is the perfect mantra for helping students with executive function problems. We know that the more we push, lecture, and punish, the more stress student brains have to handle. More stress means more emotional hijacking and less capacity to learn. So what do we need to keep in mind?

1. Identify the Causes

The first step in making student growth a reality is to carefully diagnose which barriers are standing in the way. When you assume the problem behavior is due to bad attitude or lack of effort or motivation, your reflex is to dole out consequences and forget the teaching. When you look for a reasonable cause for a student's behavior, you can be more helpful. If you cannot identify the core causes of the problem, the likelihood of choosing effective interventions is low. Using the five-step process for problem solving is an effective way to approach diagnosis. It helps demystify the problem for the student and family and gives everyone a clear focus.

2. Collaborate to Develop the Cure

Once you have identified the probable causes, explain them to the students and involve them in their goal-setting process. They need to help predict the likely results of their intervention plan. Talking things through helps students figure out what they need and how they feel so they can define and own their part of the action steps for improvement.

3. Use the Village; It Takes One

Teachers can't do the whole job alone. It takes a united effort among all the players at school and in the family for maximum growth to occur. A united effort provides consistent implementation in multiple classrooms as well as reinforcement at home. Without vigilant monitoring and follow-through, the effect never reaches its full potential.

If a student has a dysfunctional family or one hard-nosed teacher, consistency of effort may be out of your circle of influence. That doesn't mean your individual efforts are wasted; it means the students won't make the same rate of progress as they could have. Educating your peers and your students' families about executive dysfunction and how it affects students' lives can also go a long way toward creating a more supportive environment.

4. Teach Students to Self-Monitor

Often, students' reluctance to keep trying stems from an inability to judge how much progress they are actually making. Students whose success is slow need concrete representations of their personal progress. The measuring and charting of small, specific growth indicators (e.g., number of words read per minute, decrease in disruptions, increase in vocabulary) help focus students on positive results and make it easier for them to see that their efforts are paying off. Having students actively take part in setting new goals based on these data will be essential to their progress, feeling of commitment, and sense of responsibility.

5. Model, Model, Model and Then Practice, Practice, Practice

Never assume that explaining the strategy once or twice will do the trick. Repeatedly teach the skill and practice ways to apply it. You need the right amount of guided practice as well as application with different problems in different settings and corrective feedback to get students to incorporate the new skills and routines into their thinking and behavior patterns. The saying that "only perfect practice makes perfect" is a good adage, so make certain you check and recheck student understanding. Teaching skills in small-group settings, where teachers can see and hear each student's response to practice, helps catch errors and misconceptions.

6. Deliver New or Difficult Skills in Small Groups

Small-group instruction is especially important for students with weak executive functioning. Modeling and close monitoring of errors are needed because these students have a tendency to make the same mistakes over and over. Even when they have done well several times in a row, they often revert to old behaviors or make careless errors. Inconsistent performance is a hallmark of executive problems, so it is hard to know when to give guidance and when a kick in the pants would be more appropriate.

It is better to err on the side of caution and provide plenty of structure and practice than to assume the problem is due to poor effort. Only when students practice the skill, routine, or procedure so many times that it becomes automatic (not requiring conscious effort) can you count it as actually mastered. Practice followed by positive reinforcement is a winning combination.

7. Help All Students Practice Applying Executive Skills

Remember that executive skills don't fully develop until a person's mid-20s, so all students benefit from training in these areas. Some schools I work with select a specific target skill each month, and the whole school focuses on strategies that provide repeated support in the identified skill in every class, every day.

For instance, let's say the theme for the month is goal setting and planning. The art teacher demonstrates and practices using sketching as a first step of visualizing the goal before creating the project. The English teacher helps students use a rubric to score a paper from last year in order to envision exactly what the goal for quality writing looks like for this assignment. A math teacher has students first write down the steps for problem solving before actually tackling the problem for the day. The social studies teacher asks students to create a timeline of mini-tasks that will help them plan their work for completing a research project on time. Repeated application of the same basic strategy in multiple settings helps students make connections, especially if the students talk about what they are doing and why.

8. Allow for Student Rehearsal and Articulation

Teacher-centered "sage on the stage" models are effective only if the teacher spends an equal amount of class time walking around and listening to students articulate what they are learning. If I can get students to explain their own thinking so well that other students can understand the process, I know I have taught well. Instead of just giving students answers or telling them what they need to know, ask questions to see if they can come up with information on their own or use other resources. This sends them a strong message about their responsibility to learn as you support them, rather than encouraging the expectation that you are going to spoon-feed them.

Most students hate being put on the spot in front of an entire class, so this articulation process is best used when all students are participating in small groups or pairs.

9. Applaud the Effort

Even though making students live with the natural consequences of their decisions is typically a reasonable approach for a teacher to take, it often backfires for students with serious delays in executive skills. If their serious efforts reap poor results, they may believe there is no hope of getting better. In such cases, adults would be wise to set a series of smaller expectations that help students reach their goals. When teachers provide instruction that ensures student success at least 70–80 percent of the time, students will maintain the motivation to keep trying. Too much punishment or negative consequence for a beginning learner is not good practice. The term *beginning learner* describes where someone is on the learning continuum and has nothing to do with when peers learn the target skill.

For example, you wouldn't yell at a toddler for falling as he begins to learn to walk; in fact, you would encourage and support him by saying things like "Good walking!" The truth is, he is not doing "good walking" compared with an agile adult walker, but you are adjusting your expectation bar to take into account his current level of competence. As his skill builds, your level of expectation and reinforcement will change accordingly. This is not coddling or underestimating the child's ability. It is making the level of challenge reasonable enough to avoid loss of self-confidence and high stress, which actually delay progress.

Students who experience persistent failure often try to hide their embarrassment by pretending not to care. In older students, this often sounds like "This is boring, and who needs it anyway?" or "I didn't really try." Repeated failures have led them to believe that trying hard and doing what is asked aren't enough to please the adults or to feel good about accomplishments. They come to believe that giving some effort and turning in the assignment are as much as a reasonable person should expect. It is not unlike the feeling you would experience if you felt you were totally incapable of skiing down a mountain with beautiful form. Just the fact that you tried and got to the bottom without killing yourself would seem worthy of applause in your mind. Any negative lecturing talk from your instructor— "I've told you how to do this 12 times. Now try harder!"—is likely to elicit an ugly reaction from you.

When effort is followed by a positive outcome, it is more likely to be repeated, so it is important to quickly reinforce even small attempts at growth. Specific and immediate feedback has positive effects (Marzano et al., 2001). Remember, if this is a new learner in the area of executive functioning, the lack of strong skill means this student is more in an "I can't" situation than an "I won't" one, just like the toddler.

10. Don't Settle for Just a Label

Although a student may need a label to access some services at school, labels do little to identify exactly where learning or performance breaks down. Only when you identify specific barriers and missing skills can you plan appropriate short- and long-term interventions. This is not unlike when a patient complains of abdominal pain. The doctor must do more than label the problem and choose a generic remedy. Figuring out the root cause or causes of the pain is the only efficient, effective way to ensure that the intervention is appropriate. Once the cause is clear and the matching intervention decided on, it is essential that the patient (or the student, in our case) follows the plan to the letter and for the right amount of time.

If medication is part of the student intervention plan, remember that medication is only part of the solution. You don't learn new ways of acting and thinking from medication. Medication may reduce symptoms, but a carefully designed intervention plan is what provides the essential skills and habits for long-term growth.

They Can and Do Get Better

Students with executive dysfunctions often turn out to be amazingly successful adults, but they need strong support to learn to regulate and compensate for the delay of efficient firing in their brains. Trying their best won't be enough to get the job done. They need help jump-starting their processes. Once these new patterns of thinking become automatic, the positive results will reinforce their efforts and keep them growing.

Throughout this book, we have investigated ways of helping adults increase their capacity to teach students to manage their emotional and academic lives. We can't let students who struggle wear us down or wait us out. We need to take the brakes off and move them forward.

The dream most of us went into teaching with was to make a significant difference for our students. The way to do that has nothing to do with quick fixes or canned programs. It has to do with teachers who genuinely care and are always looking for better ways to help students help themselves.

BIBLIOGRAPHY

Alloway, T. P., & Alloway, R. G. (2010). Investigating the predictive roles of working memory and IQ in academic attainment. *Journal of Experimental Child Psychology, 106,* 20–29.

Alton-Lee, A., Nuthall, G., & Patrick, J. (1993, Spring). Reframing classroom research: A lesson from the private world of children. *Harvard Educational Review, 63*(1), 50–85.

Anderson, V. (1998). Assessing executive functions in children: Biological, psychological, and developmental considerations. *Neuropsychological Rehabilitation, 8*(3), 319–349.

Barkley, R. A., Murphy, K. R., & Fischer, M. (2008). *ADHD in adults: What science says.* New York: Guilford Press.

Berninger, V. W., Rutberg, J. E., Abbott, R. D., Garcia, N., Anderson-Youngstrom, M., Brooks, A., et al. (1996, February). Tier 1 and tier 2 early intervention for handwriting and composing. *Journal of School Psychology, 44*(1), 3–30.

Blair, C. (2002, February). School readiness: Integrating cognition and emotion in neurobiological conceptualization of children's functioning at school entry. *American Psychologist, 57*(2), 111–127.

Brown, T. E. (2005). *Attention deficit disorder: The unfocused mind in children and adults.* New Haven, CT: Yale University Press.

Burchers, S., Burchers, M., & Burchers, B. (1997). *Vocabulary cartoons: Building an educated vocabulary with visual mnemonics.* Punta Gorda, FL: New Monic Books.

Clark, R. C., Nguyen, F., & Sweller, J. (2006). *Efficiency in learning: Evidence-based guidelines to manage cognitive load.* San Francisco: Pfeiffer.

Cleveland Clinic. (2013). *Mind-body exercises: Harnessing the power of the mind-body connection.* Retrieved February 10, 2013, from http://my.clevelandclinic.org/heart/prevention/alternative/bodymind.aspx

Cooper-Kahn, J. D., & Dietzel, L. C. (2008). *Late, lost, and unprepared: A parents' guide to helping children with executive functioning.* Bethesda, MD: Woodbine House.

Darch, C., Carnine, D., & Gersten, R. (1984, July–August). Explicit instruction in mathematics problem solving. *Journal of Educational Research, 77*(6), 351–359.

Dean, C. H., Hubbell, E. R., Pitler, H., & Stone, B. J. (2012). *Classroom instruction that works: Research-based strategies for increasing student achievement* (2nd ed.). Alexandria, VA: ASCD.

Diamond, A. (2002). Normal development of prefrontal cortex from birth to young adulthood: Cognitive functions, anatomy, and biochemistry. In D. T. Stuss & R. T. Knight (Eds.), *Principles of frontal lobe function* (pp. 466–503). New York: Oxford University Press.

Dweck, C. (2006). *Mindset: The new psychology of success.* New York: Random House.

Elliott, J. G. (2010). An evaluation of a classroom-based intervention to overcome working memory difficulties and improve long-term academic achievement. *Journal of Cognitive Education & Psychology, 9*(3), 227–250.

Fisher, D. & Frey, N. (2008). *Better learning through structured teaching: A framework for the gradual release of responsibility.* Alexandria, VA: ASCD.

Flood, J., Lapp, D., & Fisher, D. (2005). Neurological impress methods PLUS. *Reading Psychology, 26*(2), 147–160.

Frayer, D., Frederick, W. C., & Klausmeier, H. J. (1969). *A schema for testing the level of cognitive mastery.* Madison, WI: Wisconsin Center for Education Research.

Fuchs, D., Fuchs, & L. S., & Burish, P. (2000, June). Peer-assisted learning strategies: An evidence-based practice to promote reading achievement. *Learning Disabilities Research & Practice, 15*(2), 85–91.

Fuchs, L. S., & Fuchs, D. (1986, November). Effects of systematic formative evaluation: A meta-analysis. *Exceptional Children, 53*(3), 199–208.

Fuchs, L. S., Fuchs, D., Prentice, K., Burch, M., Hamlet, C. L., Owen, R., et al. (2003, June). Explicitly teaching for transfer: Effects on third-grade students' mathematical problem solving. *Journal of Educational Psychology, 95*(2), 293–305.

Gathercole, S. E., Pickering, S. J., Knight, C., & Stegmann, Z. (2004, January). Working memory skills and educational attainment: Evidence from national curriculum assessments at 7 and 14 years of age. *Applied Cognitive Psychology, 18*(1), 1–16.

Gawande, A. (2010). *The checklist manifesto: How to get things right.* New York: Metropolitan Books.

Gersten, R., Beckmann, S., Clarke, B., Foegen, A., Marsh, L., Star, J. R., et al. (2009). *Assisting students struggling with mathematics: Response to intervention (RtI) for elementary and middle schools.* (NCEE 2009-4060). Washington, DC: National Center for Education Evaluation and Regional Assistance, Institute of Education Sciences.

Gibson, S. A. (2012). *Strategy guide: Write alouds.* Retrieved July 27, 2012, from http://www.readwritethink.org/professional-development/strategy-guides/write-alouds-30687.html

Glasser, W. (1998). *Choice theory: A new psychology of personal freedom.* New York: HarperCollins.

Goleman, D. (1995). *Emotional intelligence.* New York: Bantam.

Graham, S., Bollinger, A., Booth Olson, C., D'Aoust, C., MacArthur, C., McCutchen, D., et al. (2012, June). *Teaching elementary school students to be effective writers: A practice guide.* (NCEE 2012-4058). Washington, DC: National Center for Education Evaluation and Regional Assistance, Institute of Education Sciences. Retrieved July 16, 2012, from http://ies.ed.gov/ncee/wwc/PracticeGuide.aspx?sid=17

Graham, S., Harris, K. R., & Loynachan, C. (2012). *The basic spelling vocabulary list.* Retrieved July 18, 2012, from http://www.readingrockets.org/article/22366/

Graham, S., & Weintraub, N. (1996, March). A review of handwriting research: Progress and prospects from 1980 to 1994. *Educational Psychology Review, 8*(1), 7–87.

Hallahan, D., & Kauffman, J. M. (2000). *Exceptional learners: Introduction to special education.* Boston: Allyn and Bacon.

Hasbrouck, J., & Tindal, G. (2005). *Oral reading fluency: 90 years of measurement.* Eugene, OR: University of Oregon.

Hattie, J., Biggs, J., & Purdie, N. (1996, Summer). Effects of learning skills interventions on student learning: A meta-analysis. *Review of Educational Research, 66*(2), 99–136.

Holmes, J., Gathercole, S. E., Place, M., Dunning, D. L., Hilton, K. A., & Elliott, J. G. (2010, September). Working memory deficits can be overcome: Impacts of training and medication on working memory with children with ADHD. *Applied Cognitive Psychology, 24*(6), 827–836.

Honig, B., Diamond, L., & Gutlohn, L. (2008). *Teaching reading sourcebook* (2nd ed.). Novato, CA: Arena Press.

Hseuh-chao, M. H., & Nation, P. (2000). Unknown vocabulary density and reading comprehension. *Reading in a Foreign Language, 13*(1), 403–430.

Hughes, M., & Searle, D. (1997). *The violent E and other tricky sounds: Learning to spell from kindergarten through grade 6.* Portland, ME: Stenhouse Publishers.

Kenney, J. M., Hancewicz, E., Heuer, L., Metsisto, D., & Tuttle, C. L. (2005). *Literacy strategies for improving mathematics instruction.* Alexandria, VA: ASCD.

Lambert, N. M., & McCombs, B. L. (Eds.). (1998). *How students learn: Reforming schools through learner-centered education.* Washington, DC: American Psychological Association.

Levine, M. (2002). *A mind at a time.* New York: Simon & Schuster.

Lewis, C. H. (1982). *Using the "thinking aloud" method in cognitive interface design.* Yorktown Heights, NY: IBM.

Locke, E. A., & Latham, G. P. (2002, September). Building a practically useful theory of goal setting and task motivation: A 35-year odyssey. *American Psychologist, 57*(9), 705–717.

Marzano, R. J., Pickering, D. J., & Pollock, J. E. (2001). *Classroom instruction that works: Research-based strategies for increasing student achievement.* Alexandria, VA: ASCD.

Meichenbaum, D. H., & Goodman, J. (1971). Training impulsive children to talk to themselves: A means of developing self-control. *Journal of Abnormal Psychology, 77*(2), 115–126.

Meyer, B. J., Young, C. J., & Bartlett, B. J. (1989). *Memory improved: Reading and memory enhancement across the life span through strategic text structures.* Hillsdale, NJ: Erlbaum.

Miller, S. P., & Mercer, C. D. (1993, Spring). Using data to learn about concrete-semiconcrete-abstract instruction for students with math disabilities. *Learning Disabilities Research & Practice, 8*(2), 89–96.

National Institute of Child Health and Human Development, National Reading Panel. (2000). *Teaching children to read: An evidence-based assessment of the scientific research literature on reading and its implications for reading instruction.* (NIH Publication No. 00-4769). Washington, DC: Author.

Nauert, R. (2010, November 18). *Brain fatigue from living in the city?* Retrieved February 1, 2012, from http://psychcentral.com/news/2010/11/17/brain-fatigue-from-living-in-the-city/20993.html

Project EXSEL. (2004, May 14). *What is emotional hijack?* Retrieved February 8, 2013, from http://pd.ilt.columbia.edu/projects/exsel/aboutsel/hijack.htm

Reehm, S. P., & Long, S. A. (1996, May). Reading in the mathematics classroom. *Middle School Journal, 27*(5), 35–41.

Reeves, D. B. (2009). *Leading change in your school: How to conquer myths, build commitment, and get results.* Alexandria, VA: ASCD.

Roberts, M. (2001, July). Off-task behavior in the classroom: Applying FBA and CBM. *NASP Toolkit.* Retrieved February 1, 2013, from http://www.nasponline.org/communications/spawareness/Off-Task%20Behavior.pdf

Sadoski, M., & Paivio, A. (2001). *Imagery and text: A dual coding theory of reading and writing.* Mahwah, NJ: Erlbaum.

Schunk, D. H., & Cox, P. D. (1986). Strategy training and attributional feedback with learning disabled students. *Journal of Educational Psychology, 78*(3), 201–209.

Searle, M. A. (2007). *What to do when you don't know what to do: Building a pyramid of interventions.* Perrysburg, OH: Searle Enterprises.

Searle, M. (2010). *What every school leader needs to know about RTI.* Alexandria, VA: ASCD.

Sikström, S., & Söderlund, G. (2007, October). Stimulus-dependent dopamine release in attention-deficit/hyperactivity disorder. *Psychological Review, 114*(4), 1047–1075.

Sousa, D. A. (1998). *How the brain learns.* Thousand Oaks, CA: Corwin Press.

St. Clair-Thompson, H. L., Stevens, R., Hunt, A., & Bolder, E. (2010, March). Improving children's working memory and classroom performance. *Educational Psychology, 30*(2), 203–219.

Szalavitz, M. (2003, July/August). Tapping potential: Stand and deliver. *Psychology Today,* 50–54.

Tannen, D. (1998). *The argument culture: Moving from debate to dialogue.* New York: Random House.

Tournaki, N. (2003, September/October). The differential effects of teaching addition through strategy instruction versus drill and practice to students with and without learning disabilities. *Journal of Learning Disabilities, 36*(5), 449–558.

U.S. Department of Education. (2004). *Teaching children with attention deficit hyperactivity disorder: Instructional strategies and practices.* Washington, DC: Office of Special Education and Rehabilitative Services, Office of Special Education Programs.

Veenman, M. V., Wilhelm, P., & Beishuizen, J. J. (2004, February). The relation between intellectual and metacognitive skills from a developmental perspective. *Learning and Instruction, 14*(1), 89–109.

Vygotsky, L. (2012). *Thought and language* (Rev. and expanded ed.). Cambridge, MA: MIT Press.

Willis, J. (2010a, May 9). Want children to "pay attention"? Make their brains curious! [Blog post] Retrieved June 23, 2012, from http://www.psychologytoday.com/blog/radical-teaching/201005/want-children-pay-attention-make-their-brains-curious

Willis, J. (2010b). *Learning to love math: Teaching strategies that change student attitudes and get results.* Alexandria, VA: ASCD.

Wolfe, P. (2001). *Brain matters: Translating research into classroom practice.* Alexandria, VA: ASCD.

Wright, J. (n.d.a). *School-wide strategies for managing . . . Study skills/organization.* [Web page]. Available: http://www.interventioncentral.org/academic-interventions/study-organization/school-wide-strategies-managing-study-skills-organization

Wright, J. (n.d.b). *Sentence combining: Teaching rules of sentence structure by doing.* [Web page]. Available: http://www.interventioncentral.org/academic-interventions/writing/sentence-combining-teaching-rules-sentence-structure-doing

Zimmerman, B. J., & Schunk, D. H. (Eds.). (2001). *Self-regulated learning and academic achievement: Theoretical perspectives* (2nd ed.). Mahwah, NJ: Erlbaum.

Zins, J., Weissberg, R., Wang, M., & Walberg, H. J. (Eds.). (2004). *Building academic success on social and emotional learning: What does the research say?* New York: Teachers College Press.

INDEX

The letter *f* following a page number denotes a figure

ABOUT THE AUTHOR

Margaret Searle is the president of Searle Enterprises, Inc., an educational consulting firm. She specializes in consulting with districts and schools in the areas of curriculum alignment, differentiated instruction, inclusive education, leadership team development, and training teams to implement RTI. She also serves as an adjunct professor for Ashland University in Ashland, Ohio. Her teaching experience covers every grade from preschool through 8th grade in both a general and special education capacity. Her administrative experience has been as a K–12 supervisor in Dayton City Schools as well as a middle school principal in Springfield, Ohio, and an elementary school principal in Toledo, Ohio. She served as an advisor to President George H. W. Bush on elementary and secondary education issues.

Margaret has written three previous books, including *Standards-Based Instruction for All Learners: A Treasure Chest for Principal-Led Building Teams, What to Do When You Don't Know What to Do: Building a Pyramid of Interventions,* and *What Every School Leader Needs to Know About RTI.* Margaret is based in Perrysburg, Ohio, and may be contacted through her website (www.margaretsearle.com), by e-mail (searle@buckeye-express.com), or by phone (419-874-9505).

Related ASCD Resources: Addressing Behavior and Academic Problems

At the time of publication, the following ASCD resources were available (ASCD stock numbers appear in parentheses). For up-to-date information about ASCD resources, go to www.ascd. org. You can search the complete archives of *Educational Leadership* at http://www.ascd.org/el.

Professional Interest Communities

Visit the ASCD website and scroll to the bottom to click on "professional interest communities." Within these communities, find information about professional educators who have formed groups around topics like "Brain-Compatible Learning."

ASCD EDge Groups

Exchange ideas and connect with other educators interested in various topics, including Response to Intervention, on the social networking site ASCD EDge™.

PD Online

Classroom Management: Understanding Diverse Learning Needs, 2nd Ed. (#PD11OC110)
Response to Intervention: An Introduction (#PD11OC100)
These and other online courses are available at www.ascd.org/pdonline

Print Products

Activating the Desire to Learn by Bob Sullo (#107009)
Beyond Discipline: From Compliance to Community by Alfie Kohn (#106033)
Classroom Strategies for Helping At-Risk Students by David R. Snow (#105106)
Enhancing RTI: How to Ensure Success with Effective Classroom Instruction and Intervention by Nancy E. Frey and Douglas B. Fisher (#110037)
Getting to Got It: Helping Struggling Students Learn How to Learn by Betty K. Garner (#107024)
Inspiring the Best in Students by Jonathan Erwin (#110006)
Leading and Managing a Differentiated Classroom by Carol Ann Tomlinson and Marcia B. Imbeau (#108011)
Research-Based Strategies to Ignite Student Learning: Insights from a Neurologist and Classroom Teacher (#107006)
What Every School Leader Needs to Know About RTI by Margaret Searle (#109097)

DVDs

The Common Sense of Differentiation: Meeting Specific Learner Needs in the Regular Classroom (#605138)
Implementing RTI in Secondary Schools (#610011)
The Strategic Teacher (#610137)
Teaching Students with Learning Disabilities in the Regular Classroom (#602084)
A Visit to a Motivated Classroom (#603384)

The Whole Child Initiative

The Whole Child Initiative helps schools and communities create learning environments that allow students to be healthy, safe, engaged, supported, and challenged. To learn more about other books and resources that relate to the whole child, visit www.wholechildeducation.org.

For more information: send e-mail to member@ascd.org; call 1-800-933-2723 or 703-578-9600, press 2; send a fax to 703-575-5400; or write to Information Services, ASCD, 1703 N. Beauregard St., Alexandria, VA 22311-1714 USA.